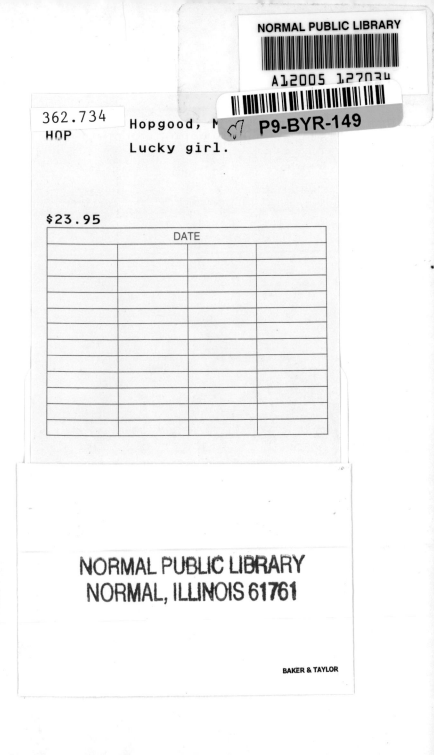

Lucky Girl

Lucky Girl

❧

MEI-LING HOPGOOD

Algonquin Books of Chapel Hill 2009

Published by

Algonquin Books of Chapel Hill

Post Office Box 2225

Chapel Hill, North Carolina 27515-2225

a division of

Workman Publishing

225 Varick Street

New York, New York 10014

Library of Congress Cataloging-in-Publication Data

Hopgood, Mei-Ling.

   Lucky girl / Mei-Ling Hopgood. — 1st ed.

     p. cm.

   ISBN-13: 978-1-56512-600-8

   1. Hopgood, Mei-Ling.   2. Hopgood, Mei-Ling—Family.
3. Taiwanese Americans—Biography.   4. Adopted children—United
States—Biography.   5. Intercountry adoption—United States—Case
studies.   6. Family—United States.   7. Birthparents—Taiwan.
8. Family—Taiwan.   9. Taiwan—Biography.   10. Taylor (Mich.)—
Biography.   I. Title.

E184.T35H67 2009

362.7340973—dc22   2008052220

10 9 8 7 6 5 4 3 2 1

First Edition

For Rollie and Chris

You find yourself in the world at all, only through an infinity of chances. Your birth depends on a marriage, or rather on the marriages of all those from whom you descend. But upon what do these marriages depend? A visit made by chance, an idle word, a thousand unforeseen occasions.

—Blaise Pascal (1623–1662)

❧ CONTENTS ❧

∾ ACKNOWLEDGMENTS ∾

I am grateful to Ma, Ba, and my Chinese family for their willingness to recount their experiences, some of which were quite painful. Special appreciation goes to all my sisters—but especially Min-Wei, Jin-Hong, and Ya-Ling—and to my brother-in-law Patrick Hafenstein for their honesty and for patiently answering, asking, and re-asking questions on my behalf and for translating to and from three languages.

Thanks to my mom, Chris Hopgood, for entertaining my constant inquisition, and to my younger siblings, Hoon-Yung and Jung-Hoe Hopgood and Irene Hofmann, for sharing their stories. My family is indebted to Sister Maureen Sinnott for making my adoption and our reunification possible.

Thank you to my editor, Andra Miller, and agents, Larry Weissman and Sascha Alper, for their guidance and for believing in the project, and to Kristina Geiser, Alexandra Salas, Kelly McMasters, Susan Ager, and Vikki Ortiz for challenging me to dig deeper.

I owe my husband, Monte Reel, endless gratitude for his good-humored affection for my family and for his encouragement, support, and invaluable feedback throughout the conception and writing of this book. He is the reason these pages saw the light of day.

Finally, I dedicate this book to my parents, Rollie and Chris Hopgood, who gave my story its happy ending.

Author's Note

I have tried to reproduce events and conversations as accurately as possible, drawing from my own memories and journals and countless conversations, letters, e-mail, and interviews with family, friends, and acquaintances. Some letters and journal entries have been edited for repetition, grammar, and punctuation.

For my biological family's history, I depended mostly on the interpretation and translation of my sisters and brother-in-law and tried to verify the facts as I understood them. For scenes and circumstances that lacked concrete or clear testimony, I re-created from imagination, and those instances are noted in the text. I have changed my birth family's Chinese surname, as well as the names of a few family members, in the interest of protecting their privacy.

↭ PROLOGUE ↭

Taoyuan, Taiwan, March 29, 1997
The luggage was coming fast. Too fast.

I stood in the baggage claim of Chiang-kai Shek International Airport, silently watching the overstuffed Samsonite suitcases, the giant cardboard boxes tied shut with red string, and the chewed-up duffel bags speed by on the conveyor belt. I was dizzy from the buzz of Mandarin—a language I could not understand—and anxious from wondering who might be waiting behind the exit door.

I was about to meet the Chinese family that gave me up for adoption days after I was born, twenty-three years earlier. During the past two months since we made first contact, I had lingered in a state of hazy, almost unnatural calm over the sudden appearance of my long-lost parents and sisters. But as I stood in the Taipei airport, I realized this reunion was real, not a dream, not just some story I might write for the newspaper I worked for. This was actually happening. To me.

Nervous and sweating, I pulled my bags off of the belt and adjusted my brown polyester shirt and skirt, an outfit I chose for its simplicity and wrinkle resistance. The rest of me looked horrible. What a grand first impression I would make: wild hair and bleary eyes, smelling of airplane funk and the smokers who puffed away during the Japan-Taiwan leg of the eighteen-hour journey. I thought my heart was going to jump out of my throat.

A perky airline employee directed me through customs and to exit 4. The doors slid open to reveal a room filled with people. They were pushing, hanging, and standing on a wood rail, waving signs in Chinese characters. They jumped up and down, wailed and shouted. I had seen my relatives in pictures, but as I scanned the Chinese faces, all of them seemed to look alike, with eyes as dark as mine.

My God. How will I know them?

Then I saw the sign, handwritten in thick, black, slanted letters: MEI-LING. A crowd of strangers rushed toward me.

I

COME BACK TAIWAN

Royal Oak, Michigan, May 1995

I had recently moved back to metro Detroit after graduating from college, and was working as a rookie reporter for the *Detroit Free Press,* writing about such cheery topics as violent teens who stalk police officers and mothers who go mad and stab their children. I rented a place on the second floor of a rickety old house smeared with a thin coat of mustard yellow paint on South Washington Avenue in the suburb of Royal Oak. I was twenty-one years old and single, so a trendy neighborhood and the abundance of nearby bars always made up for a crappy apartment. I loved my starter life, and for the first time I was feeling confident in my own skin. I believed I had conquered the insecurities over being Asian that had vexed me for so long. I thought I finally was getting a grip on who I wanted to be.

Then one afternoon, my mom called. She and Dad still lived in my hometown of Taylor, a forty-minute drive south, and now that I was back in the area we were able to chat and visit much more often. Usually we just traded mother-daughter banter on the temperamental Michigan weather, work, my brothers, my current boyfriend, and so forth, but on this day, Mom had some more interesting news to share.

"Sister Maureen called us today," she said. "She's in town and she wants to see you."

Sister Maureen Sinnott had been a distant, almost mythical figure that my parents talked about with reverence. Shortly after they married, my parents had contacted Maureen, hoping she could help them adopt a child. The nun gladly acted as the link between my birth family and my adoptive parents, maneuvering me through the maddening Taiwan and U.S. bureaucracies and caring for me for the almost eight months it took to get me out of the country. Maureen and I had exchanged letters occasionally when I was a girl, but I couldn't remember much about her.

Mom said that after many years living in other states and abroad, Maureen had returned to her native Allen Park, a Detroit suburb that borders Taylor's northeast side.

"You should call her," Mom said.

The seven or so months I had spent in Taiwan as a baby never interested me much. My birth parents were shadows, known to me only in the folds of my eyelids, the curve of my chin, or the shiny dark of my hair. They were merely characters in some child-hood fairy tale, ghosts of a former lifetime, memories that only existed because I was told they existed. The details had little to do with my happy life as an American girl who grew up with blue-eyed parents and two Korean brothers, who were also adopted. I was just another one of the endless unwanted baby girls born to and discarded by poor Chinese families. The past was the past.

Still, I was intrigued with the idea that I might meet the woman who made it possible for me to have a different life. I asked my mom for her phone number.

Maureen was bubbly, thrilled to hear that my life had turned out wonderfully.

"Oh, Mei-Ling," she said. "I'm so glad to know I made the right decision to arrange your adoption. I took care of you and I felt like a mother to you, too."

She invited me to dinner at her home.

"I have pictures," Maureen said. "Of you . . . and your mother and your father."

"You have pictures of my mother?" I asked. I had wondered, on and off, throughout my adolescence about what my mother looked like, if I had inherited my body from her, for example. For some reason, my curiosity was always focused on my birth mother, rather than my father. I never knew any photos of either existed.

"Your mother loved you, Mei-Ling. She didn't want to give you up."

Tears sprang to my eyes, catching me off guard. A surprising wave of sadness and relief washed over me. Maureen had just offered an answer to a question I never had dared to ask. *She didn't want to.* I paused before accepting the invitation for dinner. I did not want Maureen to hear my voice cracking.

MAUREEN'S ONE-BEDROOM APARTMENT in Allen Park was small, but cozy, decorated with mementos of the many years she spent globetrotting. A hand-painted scroll, a farewell gift given to her when she left Taiwan after eight years, hung on her living-room wall. She had watched a friend paint the snowy mountain scene and write in Chinese characters, "You may be leaving us, but you are leaving your footsteps behind." Maureen used an African kitenge as a tablecloth and displayed a hand-carved ebony African head purchased from an artist in Tanzania. On another wall she kept a large framed profile of an African woman with a tear running down her cheek. Maureen said she bought the picture at an ethnic festival in Detroit about twenty years ago and took it wherever she went because, to her, it symbolized all who are oppressed.

I recognized Maureen only a little from old black-and-white pictures my parents had shown me. She had been thirty-one years old when she cared for me. Back then, she was quite thin and kept her hair tucked under her veil. The modern, in-living-color Maureen was age fifty-four, short and robust. Her dark, wavy hair was uncovered and she wore pants and a purple sweater over a blue and white shirt. She had sharp blue eyes that welled up with tears when she saw me. We hugged like old friends.

"It is so good to see you," Maureen said. "You turned out so well."

She introduced me to Sister Shirley Smith, who also had helped care for me at St. Mary's Hospital. The three of us sat on Maureen's couch, drank tea, and chatted about my blossoming career as a journalist and Maureen's world adventures and new psychology practice. Maureen cooked a chicken and veggie stir-fry dinner, which we ate with chopsticks. After our meal, Maureen took out an envelope filled with dozens of photos she had taken in Taiwan, of St. Mary's hospital, of the nurses, of my birth family. We examined each while Maureen and Shirley reminisced, laughing at how young and skinny they were back then.

In one picture, Maureen holds me as I reach down to pull the hair of one of my sisters. My grandmother, an auntie, and Shirley stand nearby. In another, also taken the day I left Taitung, Maureen and I pose with several nurses and my birth parents, who had come to say good-bye. I am in Maureen's arms, but my biological mother stands nearby, resting her hand on my arm. Her hair is pulled back and she is wearing a striped sweater over a yellow button-down shirt and red shoes. My birth father stands to Maureen's right, partially cut out of the frame. He is wearing a brown jacket. I didn't see myself in either of them. I examined the way my mother touched me — her face seemed almost expressionless — and wondered what she must have felt.

At the end of the evening, Maureen said, "You know, Mei-Ling, if you ever want to contact your birth family, I am sure they would be exactly in the same place you left them."

I stared at her. It was the first time that the possibility of searching for my biological family—and the prospect that I might actually *find* them—had crossed my mind seriously. While I was growing up, when anyone would ask me if I wondered what became of them, I'd answer no. No, I did not know how many siblings I had. No, I did not know much about Taiwan. No, I did not care to meet them. As a teenager, I practically took pride in my ignorance.

I mean, why dwell on the past? A choice was made for my good or theirs, or for both, and ultimately, as soon as I was poured into the arms of Rollie and Chris Hopgood one April afternoon in 1974, these two midwestern teachers became my real family. They read me bedtime stories, attended my recitals, helped me build homecoming floats, and took me on vacations to Florida. My mom dressed me in pretty clothes and drove me to dance class; I admired her pale, slender beauty and her measured patience, even when our opposite personalities clashed. My dad took me grocery shopping, to the dances he chaperoned, and on the picket lines when he led strikes. I was just like him, strong-willed, independent, and passionate; our battles shook the windows, but we were fiercely devoted to each other. Hoon-Yung and Jung-Hoe, who were both adopted from South Korea, were my real brothers, my playtime companions. I taught Hoon-Yung to play house and camp out and helped Jung-Hoe speak English and sleep on a bed. Instead of enduring poverty and prejudice against girls and women, I had been raised to believe I could do anything that I wanted. I had a close family, a rich life, and the endless opportunities of the great United States of America.

I'm lucky, I've always told myself.

Perhaps one day I might like to know more about these figures from my past and the reasons they made the decisions that they did. One day. But not today.

I thanked Maureen for the suggestion but told her I'd have to think about it.

"Maybe if you want to write to the hospital in Taitung," I suggested, "just to see if the nurses know where my family is? But not to contact them . . . Just to see . . ." I said.

Because my response was less than enthusiastic, Maureen decided to wait. Not long afterward, I left Detroit, chased away by a labor strike at my newspaper. I moved to St. Louis and started another reporting job. I had a great group of fun friends. We were young and ambitious, spending our days dissecting other people's stories, but I still had little interest in digging into my own.

In late 1996 I was jotting down a holiday note to Maureen when I remembered our conversation from the year before. I wondered if she had ever written to St. Mary's to confirm the whereabouts of my family. I casually asked, "Did you ever write to the hospital?"

Maureen interpreted my question as a request: *Write to the hospital.* And she did.

BARELY A MONTH LATER, on January 26, 1997, I was folding phyllo dough into triangles, getting ready for a cocktail party at my apartment in the Central West End neighborhood of St. Louis. I had fussed over a simple menu: bagel chips with hummus, veggies, spanikopita, quiches, dips and chips, the usual party fare. The house reeked of slightly burnt cooking oil, and my kitchen was a mess. Pans, knives, opened packages, strips of phyllo dough, and cut vegetables were piled on my counter. My dog waited expectantly at my feet, hoping to profit from the disorder and my general sympathy for her forlorn face. I planned to play jazzy tunes, serve martinis, and wear a short purple velvet dress bought at a secondhand store. We would talk some shop— lamenting missed deadlines and dreadful assignments—but mostly we would laugh and tell stories about crazy politicians, bad dates, about our families and our quirky midwestern hometowns.

I was far behind schedule, frantic, and covered in flour, when the phone rang. I wiped my sticky fingers on a towel and grabbed the receiver.

"Hello?"

It was Maureen.

"Mei-Ling," she said, her voice bubbling with excitement. "I have a letter from the hospital."

A nun at St. Mary's had sent her information about my birth family.

"Both mother and father are from Kinmen. The father is fifty-nine years old, while the mother is fifty-four," Maureen read. "The occupation of the father is a farmer. Mother, a housewife."

The letter recited a laundry list of dry statistics with no names from a family on the other side of the world: "First female, married, a government-employed researcher . . ." In all, there were seven siblings in Taiwan, six sisters and one brother whom they had adopted. One more daughter, the youngest, had been given up for adoption to a couple in Switzerland.

I froze, leaning hard on my kitchen counter.

My mother and father? My sisters and brother?

Maureen read on: "The father is excited to see Mei-Ling. He is inviting her if she could come on Chinese New Year, which will be on February 7, 1997. He said the children do come at this time." He had included a business card and a self-addressed envelope.

"Can you believe it?" she asked.

I couldn't—I was shocked. I think I said something like "Wow! That's amazing."

Still, I didn't want this strange news to crowd my busy life. There were too many unknowns, and deep down I was a little afraid of being too curious. I preferred *not* caring about my biological past. What if I was disappointed or hurt by what I discovered? Maureen told me she'd forward me the letter, and we could decide what to do next.

Dazed and unbelieving, I called my parents. They were excited and eager to know more. I recounted the story again to friends who came over that night. We oohed and ahhed, and speculated about what it all might mean. An Asian American colleague pointed out that my family had appeared at the turn of the Chinese Year of the Ox, in which we both were born.

"They waited until our year to find you," she marveled. We raised our glasses and toasted this revelation. I felt elated and strange, with only a vague sense that much of what I knew about who I was and what I believed about my past and future was about to change.

I ARRIVED HOME FROM a business trip in Kansas City a few days later. My Chinese Shar-Pei, Delilah, greeted me with her customary dance of twists and turns and tail wags. I stretched one hand down to pat her wrinkles, still wearing my coat. I shuffled absent-mindedly through the mail and then reached over and pushed the button on the answering machine sitting on the edge of the kitchen counter.

Beep.

It was Maureen, breathless with news again. She had another letter, this time from one of my sisters. She read it to my machine:

Dear Mei-Ling,

How are you for these years? We are missing you. When we know your news we are very glad. And especially Father and Mother. I'm your elder sister. Father and Mother want to see you in a hurry. They hope you can back Taiwan in New Year

'97. *Father say he want to buy the ticket for you if you want to come Taiwan so if you receive my letter please reply as soon as to me. We expect your good news.*
    Your elder sister, Joanna

This was all happening so fast. These people were threatening to jump off of the page and into my life.

Maureen sent me the original letter from Joanna, my second-oldest sister, whose actual name is Jin-Qiong. My sister had written on rice paper that crinkled to touch, delicate and exotic. The envelope was written in Chinese, except for the words *Taitung, Taiwan.*

About a week later, I received another letter from another sister. In that envelope were tucked a few photographs. I pulled them out and examined them closely, holding the photos not far from my nose to get a good look at each person. I scrutinized eyes, faces, lips, and bodies. Who was taller? Who was prettier? Who looked the most like me, my mother or father? Which sister? Some of the pictures were old, dating back to my last days in Taiwan, variations of those I had seen at the home of Sister Maureen almost two years earlier. Those baby photos did not surprise or move me this time, but the more recent photos did—especially a family portrait taken at the wedding of one my sisters.

The picture was a few years old. In it, the bride wears a red and gold dress, a jade pendant, and sparkly, dangling earrings. Her hair is pinned up, and a few tight spirals frame her face. She is pale, heavily made up, and her lips are parted in a demure smile. Almost twenty relatives, sisters in dresses, brothers-in-law in suits, aunts, uncles, and cousins, press in close, standing on tiptoes, contorting their necks and backs, trying to fit in the frame. I noted that many of the women, presumably my sisters, wore the same bright red shade of lipstick. My tiny grandmother, my father's mother, sits serenely front and center wearing a shiny blue silk shirt. Her hands rest on her knees and a cane is propped beneath her right armpit. She has what looks like a receding white hairline and reminded me of some character out of an old Kung Fu movie, an old and wise prophet about to bestow a secret to a worthy disciple. My mother sits to her right, wearing a pink and white checkered suit, white hose, heels, and a corsage with a red ribbon pinned to her chest. Her hair is permed and bobbed, and her bangs are teased into a perfect curl on her forehead. Her mouth, too, is painted in the same bright red, and she is grinning, but she is caught with her eyes shut. To her right is my only slightly smiling father, stern and straight, handsomely dressed in a Western suit with a colorful tie held in place with a tie pin. He also wears a flower with a red ribbon imprinted with gold Chinese characters. On the back of the photo is written, "The grandma is dead (21 May 1996), 86 years old. The picture is taken in the occasion of the 4th daughter's marriage."

At the time, I didn't know who was who in this family portrait, save the bride, my parents, and grandmother. The group seemed a joyful jumble of chaos. It was odd knowing that these strangers were directly related to me, but what struck me most was the realization that my siblings were not merely the children of a poor farming family, as I had believed. If I had an image of my birth family at all in my head, it had been in black and white and dismal. They would be gaunt, wearing ragged clothes and probably standing in some barren field with a shabby, straw-roofed hut at their backs, a stereotypical portrait of third-world poverty. I mean, that was why they had given me up for adoption, right?

Yet that was not who they were. Perhaps they were before, but not now. They were a middle-class family. My sisters were attractive, educated, and successful. What few assumptions I had were wrong.

"They all look like they love each other very much," I wrote in my journal.

I had never cared about them before or even thought of them as real people. I never had—nor did I seek—enough information to feel a connection with my biological origins. My mom and dad told me what they knew, and I never sought to know more. This was probably both a conscious and unconscious decision. You are less likely to mourn those you do not realize you have lost—or those who have lost you. You do not yearn for a life that you don't know exists. Now I not only knew what I had gained from being adopted, but I suddenly was beginning to see what I had missed, and I wanted to know more.

I hurriedly dug up a few pictures of my own. I sent one of my family, one of my dog and me, and another taken in Hawaii of me with some friends. In the latter, I'm tan, wearing a sarong and a red and white checkered shirt and sitting on a couch with my friend Monica and her pals the week before her wedding in Honolulu. I chose that picture because of my smile, which was wide, and my eyes—they didn't look squinty or crooked as they occasionally did in pictures. These would be the first images of the modern-day me that they would see, and I wanted to look good. I sent the letters global priority mail to Taiwan, one to my sister and one to my parents.

"Dear Mother and Father," I wrote. "I received your letter and I'm overjoyed to find you. I'm very sorry I cannot come to Taiwan for Chinese New Year, but I want to come soon. How have you been through these years?"

In a short and polite note, I went on to describe in brief my life as a young journalist. Nothing too revealing or complicated. Nothing they couldn't understand. Then I signed off, "Love, your daughter, Mei-Ling."

. . .

THE NEXT FRIDAY I left for Mardi Gras in New Orleans in a rented van with friends from the newspaper. We marauded all weekend in the French Quarter before driving back to St. Louis on Monday, exhausted. After dropping off the rental, I drove my Saturn home. My ugly little apartment complex, a nondescript blob of brick buildings that had managed to skirt the neighborhood's zoning laws, was surrounded by magnificent early twentieth-century stone homes and Victorian mansions. I lugged my bags upstairs, ready to collapse in bed. The door opened to the living room, which still had that mismatched college look—a white couch, a green futon, and an on-again, off-again peace lily wilting by the window.

This time, I found several messages on my answering machine. At first I thought they were pranks because the callers did not say anything, although there were loud, unintelligible voices in the background.

Then in a later message, a timid, rather high voice said, "I'm your younger sister Taiwan." Click.

In another, a woman's voice in English, presumably a nun from St. Mary's hospital, said, "Mei-Ling. Your mother and father want to talk to you. They tried to call you several times."

They tried to call me.

I couldn't think about it. I was too tired to process what was happening. It seemed like some bizarre dream. *Try to relax*, I thought. I had to try to go on with my normal life, which meant work early the next day. I went to bed.

In the morning, two faxes in perfect English that had arrived over the weekend were delivered to my desk at work. They were letters from my "mother" and "father," though obviously someone else had written on their behalf.

"We all miss you very much," they said. "We hope we can hear you as soon as possible."

Even a nun from an order in St. Louis left a message on my work voice mail. This woman I did not know told me my family was trying to get ahold of me and that I should try to call them. I shook my head in amazement.

Jeez. The whole world is trying to find me.

THEY REACHED ME at about eleven thirty that night.

"Wang Mei-Ling?" a woman asked.

Um. No one had ever called me that, but obviously they were referring to me.

"Um," I said.

"Wang Mei-Ling?" Hollering in the background.

"Yes?" I said.

"YES?" I repeated loudly, for they seemed neither to hear nor understand me for all the background noise.

"This is your family Taiwan. I am Joanna Wang, your elder sister."

"How are you?" I asked, not sure what else to say.

"You speak Chinese?"

"No, I'm sorry."

The conversation was chaotic. I tried to extract as much information as I could even though we could barely understand each other. Sisters and brothers-in-law passed the phone to each other, one after another. I could not keep track of whom I was talking to, even though I tried to take notes. In the end, the conversation went something like this:

"So many your sisters want talk to you," a man said. "We got your pictures. They are very pretty. You are beautiful."

"You all are, too!"

Change of callers. "I am your sister."

"Hello," I said, laughing nervously.

"You look like me," she said. "Do you receive our fax?"

"Yes," I said. "Where are you?"

"Taitung. All of us sister go home to visit Chinese New Year. Tomorrow we must go to work. Do you work today?"

"Yes, it's not a holiday here," I said.

"Do you want to hear Papa's voice? He cannot speak English."

"Okay . . ." I started to say, but the phone was already changing hands.

A man said, "*Ni hao,*" which means "hello."

"*Ni hao,*" I said. At least I could say that much, because my parents had named my childhood cat Ni Hao (pronounced nee-how).

He said something else, but I did not understand. Shocked and dazed, I laughed again, not knowing what else to do. *My father . . .* another sister grabbed the phone.

"He want to see your visit," she said. "Do you heard of Taipei?"

"Yes," I said.

"There is also Hsinchu, where I live. I live near airport in Taipei. I am elder sis-tah. I am thirty-five," said Jin-Feng, my oldest sister. "Mama want to hear your voice. You want to talk Mama?"

"Okay . . ."

Mumbling, rustling, laughing in the background.

"Mei-Ling-ah! *Wo shi nida mama.*"

"*Ni hao!*" I said, giggling again. I heard the frantic excitement in her voice and felt a catch, a longing in my chest. I wanted to savor the moment—one that I never expected to happen—but it was pushed aside by the next sister. "She say she is your mother. She is happy! Mama can't speak English . . . Papa want to see a recent picture. That picture you send was two years ago. "

"Okay," I said.

More shrieking laughter in the background.

"You want come Taiwan? We hope you can come Taiwan. You want come Taiwan? We want to see you now. We plan together in April . . . To memory our past grandmother . . . You do the best to come. We can all be together."

"Sure," I said, caught up in the moment.

"You fax a letter with your travel plans," she said. "It's very nice hearing our news and hear your voice. We see you soon. We are missing you. Bye!"

"Okay, bye." Click.

I hung up and shook my head as if I had just been bonked with a big dodgeball. I just heard the voices of my birth parents, my sisters, and who-knows-who-else for the first time. It had happened so quickly, in such a blur. I was breathless and giddy, unsure of what I was feeling. What an odd thing to be treated with such familiarity. We had giggled out of excitement, nervousness, and frustration over the language barrier.

Wild. They called me Wang Mei-Ling. I had just told them I would try to visit them in Taiwan, didn't I?

What was I getting myself into?

THE LETTERS, E-MAIL, and faxes continued. I could tell the Wangs wanted desperately to meet me, to be reassured that they had done the right thing so long ago.

"I have to tell you that we all love you very much. Father send you to your adopted parents for some reasons. I think you do not blame him, do you?" wrote Jin-Zhi, another older sister. I didn't, but I had hoped to take my time getting to know them, to advance slowly into these uncharted waters.

However, my Chinese family had only one speed: *kuai*. Fast.

"Come home," they pleaded.

My American parents were nothing but supportive. In fact,

they encouraged me to pursue the relationship. My dad later told me, "We knew this was not the end of our chapter in your life; it was just the beginning of a new one."

Yet I had misgivings. Taiwan was not my home. My biological parents and I were joined by blood and I willingly called them Mother and Father, and myself their daughter, but we did not know each other. I did not speak Taiwanese or Mandarin, their native languages. We may share genes, but we came from different cultures, different worlds. Sure, a reunion might be joyous, therapeutic, and moving.

But there was always the chance that I would return to the place of my birth and see my face in their faces, but we would make no connection. Or even worse, the blissful slumber would have been broken, the Pandora's box of the House of Wang would fly open and the ghosts of regret and sorrow would spew forth. As a reporter, I understood how tragic family secrets could be once unleashed. I knew that asking questions could open wounds and disrupt the course of once-peaceful lives. Sometimes ignorance really is bliss. Sometimes there are puzzles better left unsolved, so that life can be allowed to heal and move on. Yet my own mystery seemed to be unraveling at breakneck speed—no matter what I had to say about it.

Some people spend their whole lives trying to uncover, understand, or escape from their pasts. Mine rose up like a dragon, fast and furious. And I was blissfully ignorant, a sleeping ox about to be discovered—and devoured.

2

THE BIRTH OF A FAMILY

Kinmen Island, August 1958

Wang Xi stood in the courtyard of his family home in the village of Xi Yuan (West Garden) making tofu, following the ritual he knew by heart.

During the hot summer months, the teenager woke up early, well before sunrise. He soaked fresh soybeans for four to five hours and then boiled them. He pulverized the swollen bean casings and separated the curds of soy milk. He strained the goopy mixture through a piece of cheesecloth, stirred in a thickener called *shigaofen* and covered it with a lid. An hour or two later, he poured the beans into a mold where the mixture would harden.

Tofu was the lifeblood of the Wang family; they made their living selling it to villagers and soldiers. Their customers ate it raw, dried, or deep-fried. They liked to eat boiled bean curd in the morning, with bits of scallions and soy sauce, or sprinkle tofu cubes in fish soup. Some liked to snack on pressed tofu or strips boiled in special sauces, such as a strong tea or a mixture of cinnamon, cumin, and cloves. Others liked tofu soaked in the fermented brine of vegetables or seafood, served with a spicy sauce. A good bowl smelled not unlike garbage rotting in the sun.

Standing over an old wooden table, the mundane task seemed

custom-made for daydreaming. A teenager like Xi could easily get lost in his thoughts, in fantasies, like one day starting a business that would earn lots of money and end his family's need to walk in flimsy sandals from village to village hawking tofu, cucumbers, onions, and peanuts. Perhaps he would even build a grand house and own an automobile. He'd choose a good wife who would take care of him and his parents during the days and heat his bed during the nights. She would have many children, and most certainly boys. The first son would be thick and healthy, with a voice of steel, crying like an emperor on the day he is born. They would be brilliant parents, and unlike himself, his children would finish school, maybe even college, and go on to work in jobs that earned in one month, a hundred, even a thousand times what he earned in a year. They would be smart, ambitious, and passionate like him, but above all obedient. One day the young man hoped he would be a worthy father.

But daydreams could not last long, not with the bombs.

It started as a whisper, a slight whistle like that of a distant bird, but it quickly mushroomed into an ear-piercing screech— *Shooo!*—and then a deafening roar. Next came the shaking earth and the falling trees or walls or roofs, and all the smoke and dust, and screams and sometimes blood and carnage.

There was always that pause between the sound and the fury, the seconds before the shells found their marks, when the air congealed and time contracted. Those were the most exasperating, thrilling, terrifying moments—those seconds that the gods took to decide their fate.

China began a forty-four-day bombardment of Kinmen, an almost constant barrage of shells and artillery. Xi did not run. It was far too late; his fate was upon him.

Two bombs struck, blowing rock and dirt high into the air. Walls and parts of ceilings collapsed in piles of cement and dust.

The earth trembled for what seemed like hours, days, weeks after, and despite endless efforts to repair it, his neighborhood would be scarred forever, with burns in the walls and holes in the ground.

The shells landed in the front and back of Xi's house, but somehow he lived. In fact, he was unhurt. He stood among the pulsing, smoking, shifting rubble, dazed but untouched.

Guanyin, the Divine Mother of Buddhism, giant and benevolent, had smiled upon him. It was an unforgettable brush with immortality, a taste of the kind he hoped to sustain one day, when his loyal sons worshipped at his graveside. But for now, he had escaped death, and he thanked the gods for that.

A very special place you have to visit is your ancestors' homeland, Kinmen Island. —Fax from my birth father, February 24, 1997

I always thought I knew where I had come from: *The daughter of a poor farming family in Taiwan.* The fact that my birth parents, Wang Xi and Yang Shu, were actually from Kinmen—wherever that was—was the first of many revelations, big and small, that began to debunk the history I had thought was mine. After reading that first mention of Kinmen in the first letter I ever received from my family, I combed the Internet, encyclopedias, and atlases for more information and found very little. I did discover that Kinmen, also known as Quemoy, was actually a spray of about a dozen islets nestled in the Taiwan Strait barely a mile and a half off the coast of southern China. About fifty thousand people lived there.

My ancestors were among the many immigrants from neighboring Fujian Province who moved to Kinmen, importing their language, culture, and customs. They spoke Holo, a dialect from

Southern Fujian that is now more commonly known as Taiwanese because of its pervasiveness there, and built colorful concrete housing complexes with open-air courtyards. Red-tiled roofs were shaped like swallow tails, sloping gently downward in the center but curving sharply upward to two opposing peaks. The islands were a place of tradition and strict Confucian values, thanks to scholars who proselytized there during imperial times.

During the earliest years of my parents' childhood, Kinmen was the peaceful and poor domain of farmers and fisherman. The people lived off of every root, seed, and crop that the soil would yield and every kind of fish and crustacean their nets could snag. They accented their meals with fiery rice liquor that instantly flushed faces and seared nasal membranes. Their hands were rough and their language coarse. They laughed and talked loudly, often sounding as if they were fighting. Children rarely finished school because they were needed in the fields. Life was hard but straightforward: a blunt knife against stone.

Throughout history, Kinmen had attracted its share of pirates, explorers, aspiring and deposed dictators, and gallant rebels. Emperors built walls and moats and set up a hundred-household garrison post there during the early Ming dynasty, hoping to protect China from Japanese marauders. Thus the islands earned the name Kinmen, the Golden Gate or the "impenetrable gateway." Kinmen's main claim to fame was its role as the last piece of Chinese land that the Nationalists were able to hang on to when the Communists drove them out of Mainland China in 1949.

My father was eleven and my mother six when Mao Zedong and his Communist revolution chased Nationalist leader Chiang Kai-shek and his millions of Kuomintang followers out of China and into Taiwan. On his way, Chiang grabbed hold of Kinmen and refused to let go, converting the islands into his last stand and the final line of defense for the Nationalists.

Soldiers overran the place. They hollowed mountains to hide their ships and constructed fierce steel barriers offshore. They buried mines in the beaches and dug a maze of bunkers and tunnels beneath the soil. They covered rocks on the coast where children once climbed with jagged multicolored glass, hoping invading amphibious Communist warriors would be sliced to pieces. The military opened hospitals, brothels, and cemeteries and was the industry, customer, protector, and destroyer of Kinmen. Still, the people adapted. They learned to fold violence and uncertainty into everyday life, to recognize the sound of the approaching bombs. Narrow escapes became part of the local lore, and the men puffed out their chests in pride when they told stories about cheating death. The people of Kinmen started making their living off the conflict, selling vegetables, tofu, cigarettes, rooms, sex. A soldier's money was as good as any.

Sometimes life even felt normal. And so it did, even in the predawn hours of August 23, 1958, when my father arose to make the day's batch of tofu.

Ma recalled working happily in a vegetable patch she had planted roadside. She had quit school after she finished first grade. Her job, as the second-oldest daughter in a family that would eventually include four sons and five daughters, was simple, cut from the Confucian mantra. She would be a dutiful daughter, wife, and mother, and she would follow what was expected of her to the end.

I like to picture Ma as she might have been on Kinmen, a teenager with thick hair pulled back out of her face, the first whispers of morning light kissing her ruddy cheeks and forehead. Her feet would be damp from dew and her nails dark from planting and picking. Kinmen, despite its poverty, could be a sublime place, a green oasis in the shadow of the Red Kingdom. The islands were a maze of plateaus, lakes, mangrove forests, wetlands, and waterfalls. Just offshore, granite rocks jutted out of the crashing ocean. Blue-tailed bee eaters and magpie robins flitted among the violet and white flowers in full summer bloom. Ma might have enjoyed this daily escape, away from the demands of her parents and the prattle of her siblings, lost in her own patch of dirt. On the morning of August 23, she and a neighbor friend were work-ing together in her garden, laughing, gossiping, and enjoying the fresh air and each other's company.

Around 6:30 a.m. the whistle, scream, and roar of what seemed like a million bombs shattered the serenity of their morning. The blue sky ripped into fiery shreds. Ma started to run. She ran and ran and ran as explosions disintegrated the trees and gorged the land around her. The Communists were attacking. On Ba's home, in Ma's quiet patch, everywhere.

Whole villages were destroyed and burned. She ran to a bomb bunker, fearing for her life, but in the end her whole family man-aged to survive.

A thousand civilians and soldiers died in that barrage of 475,000 shells that locals call the forty-day war, but like her future husband, somehow Ma lived. The gods had looked favor-ably upon her, too.

"THE FIRST THING you have to know, the most impor-tant thing you must know," my Chinese tutor proclaimed, "is food.

"*Mifan,*" she said, soft then hard, as if starting a song. "Rice." She drew a little bowl of rice on her notepad.

"*Mifan,*" I babbled, forgetting it as soon as I said it. I jotted a phonetic, Romanized translation in a notebook. Mee-fahn.

I knew only the barest basics about the Chinese people from my American parents who had tried to expose me to Chinese culture. What I knew I mostly learned from books, movies, and Chinese American friends. I had read Asian American classics,

such as *Joy Luck Club* and *Woman Warrior*. I could use chopsticks and say "hello." I knew that many Chinese parents put
an incredible amount of pressure on their children to succeed in
school. I knew bowing was a sign of respect and that red was an
auspicious color.

I also knew I would need to learn a lot more if I wanted to
really connect with my birth family. As soon as I began corresponding with my sisters, I studied as much as I could about
Chinese history, customs, and language. A couple of St. Louis
University students from Taiwan agreed to be my tutors, and we
met once every week in their apartments, which always seemed
to smell of warm tea and simmering garlic. They were friendly,
kind, and funny, always offering me food and drink and never
charging me for a class.

During my first lesson, Chia-Ling explained the importance
of knowing about food. She served me tea and Pepsi because she
had learned that Americans like to drink cold drinks (unlike the
Taiwanese) and was eager to put this knowledge to use.

Chinese culture revolved around food, she explained. It expressed love, hospitality, generosity, gratefulness, reverence,
modesty, despair, and so forth.

"You should learn how to say, 'I'm full,'" she said. "That's
very important. *Wo chi baole.*"

Oooh. That one's harder.

"*Wo . . .*" I began.

"*Wo chi baole,*" she prodded.

"Whoo sure bow-la." I felt like I was speaking with a mouthful of marbles.

She shook her head.

"*Wo CHI baole.*"

"*Wo chi baole,*" I managed. Little did I know how useful that
sentence would be.

I should have studied Mandarin during college, I thought. I

had chosen Spanish instead, flown to Mexico, become infatuated with the warmth of Latin families, and sizzled on the beaches of Mazatlán and Puerto Vallarta. I remember, before choosing my study abroad program, seeing the red flyers for a two-year language program in China next to the green Mizzou-to-Mexico brochures. I deliberately passed over the red ones. I always hated then how people assumed I should speak Chinese just because I looked Chinese. I spent so many years trying to defy stereotype that I all but ignored my heritage. Now I was paying for it.

Thank goodness my tutors were patient. They taught me to say the essentials, such as "thank you," "I have to go to the bathroom," and "I want a cup of beer." They served me rich and immaculately wrapped pineapple cakes, and we practiced Mandarin inflection by saying the name of that delicacy.

"*Fenglishu.*" Pineapple cake.

I moved my head in exaggerated motions trying physically to force my voice to imitate the tones. *Feng:* head down abruptly, cutting short the syllable. *Li:* tip head back while voice climbs upward. *Shu:* move head side to side while voice stays suspended on high note. I asked my tutors to teach me specific sentences, such as "I am your daughter" and "I am glad to be home" and "I love you." I made lists of words, and rewrote those lists. I tried to summon some deep-seated recollection of my first days alive, when I lived in St. Mary's hospital and the nurses cooed to me. Nothing.

I knew I couldn't recover a lifetime of language in a matter of days. I didn't even realize that because my parents were from Kinmen, they spoke Taiwanese first. Nor did I consider that although they spoke Mandarin, the barriers that separated us went far deeper than language. I would have to be content with stumbling my way through this experience, depending on others to tell me what was happening and hope that nothing important got lost or hidden in translation.

Father said you were very beautiful when he saw the pictures
of yours. We all believe that, because your mother are also a
beauty. —E-mail from Jin-Zhi, February 16, 1997

BY 1960 KINMEN was a safer place to live, though
China still shelled the islands on odd-numbered days. Mostly, the
Communists would drop propaganda bombs, fierce words stuffed
in a metal shell. Instead of blowing people to bits, the containers
exploded into a confetti shower of leaflets urging the Nationalists to surrender and telling the people of Kinmen that China was
great and Taiwan was miserable. The shrapnel from these shells
could blind eyes, scar faces and hands and scald necks, but usually the villagers could escape death. When the dust settled, they
brushed themselves off and checked their limbs and those of their
loved ones, and went back to farming or drying peanuts on the
walkways outside their homes. The Kinmenese would collect the
shrapnel and make knives; the metal was strong and sharp enough
to cut through almost anything.

Ma and her family briefly moved to Taiwan to escape the bomb-
ings, but after about a year, my grandfather decided to return. This
was the cycle of my ancestors. They were always running to and
from things: seeking peace during war, a job when their children
had nothing to eat, a piece of land to farm when drought sucked
the life from the earth or when floods saturated it, a luckier mahjong table. Most were never able to escape the poverty that had
dogged them like a birth defect passed down from generation to
generation. They moved many times chasing dreams of money or
a better life, but they almost always returned to Kinmen.

Thus, Ma was in her village of Guan Ao on the fateful day
that my birth father came to sell vegetables there. He was twenty-
three, and she was eighteen. Someone pointed her out: *She is*
single and of marrying age.

Ba did not speak to her, and she did not notice him. Decades later, he would not remember that first encounter, or at least chose not to acknowledge that any enchanted moment passed between them. He would not even admit to any attraction, but something must have drawn him to her because he asked a matchmaker to arrange a meeting. Ma was blossoming into a curvy young woman with long black hair, smooth skin, and a contagious smile. Most of all, she was docile and a hard worker, essential qualities in a future wife. Ba decided he liked her and asked her father's consent for marriage.

Ma told me that she thought that Ba was handsome, with a lean, strong face. He was charismatic, though serious, with a charming smile. (She shakes her head now as she recounts her infatuation with qualities that today seem meaningless to her.) Ba seemed to be a good, responsible man: a good Confucian. At the time, he was shouldering the difficult role of being head of his household because the year before his father died from a horse kick to the stomach and his older brother had moved to Singapore. Thus, the responsibility of caring for his mother and younger brother fell to him. He and his mother agreed that he needed a wife who could help out.

Ma's father was anxious to marry off his daughter: a son-in-law (i.e., the dowry) was a potential windfall. Ma's father liked Ba's cleverness and ambition, though Ba would never provide the money his father-in-law hoped for. My grandfather consented to their marriage. No one asked Ma what she wanted, and though she could have protested, she did not. Silent acquiescence was her response and, many decades later, her regret.

Ma wore a simple white dress when she married Ba in 1961 in his family home in the village of West Garden, before a small audience of family. Ma must have been a gorgeous bride, the glow of promise flushing her face. As she bowed before the ancestral shrine of her new family, she might have prayed that she would be a good wife who would meet the expectations of her husband and her mother-in-law, that they would work hard together and be rewarded with money and plenty of children, especially boys. Maybe she would even be happy. Indeed, within months of their marriage, Ma became pregnant, and her belly grew round and taut.

Why our parents gave you up. There are many reasons. First, all of the traditional Chinese consider that to have a boy is better than a girl. Our father is very traditional man, and he was affect deeply by Chinese culture and socity. If you do understand the past culture of Chinese, you will find that girls had being considered, "Nothing." —Letter from Jin-Zhi, spring 1997

Ba and Ma had their first child, my eldest sister, in the Year of the Tiger, November 1962. They used the first character from the word Kinmen, to create her name: Jin-Feng. (Kin and Jin are different Romanizations of the same Chinese character 金, which means gold.) Less than two years later, in April 1964, the Year of the Dragon, came the birth of a second daughter, Jin-Qiong. Both girls were healthy, born in auspicious years, but what Ba wanted more than anything was a son.

Ba himself had been one of nine sons—though only three survived childhood—and believed that the survival of the family depended on the birth of a male heir. Only a son could be counted on to support the parents when they were old. Only a son should inherit any family business, the family home, and the family fortune. Only a son could perpetuate the name and bloodline, and worship and care for a father's spirit properly.

In China, male superiority has been handed down dynasty

after dynasty, reinforced by the teachings of Confucius, Mencius, and countless other scholars, then perpetuated by fathers and mothers alike. Common Chinese were incredibly adept at finding spectacular new ways to reenforce the patrilineal belief system and destroy female self-worth for generations. Men have married and remarried and taken extra wives all in pursuit of this goal. At worst, they even have raped, abused, kidnapped and killed, all with the nod of both legal and social acceptance. Not to be outdone, women have conducted atrocities almost as often as the men; the social constructs of society encouraged it. Women ruled households when they bore boys and became worthless wives and concubines if they did not. They abused daughters-in-law who did not produce sons and sold away their daughters. They have been killed and have committed suicide. They have abandoned, drowned, and suffocated their children to punish themselves and get back at their husbands.

True, time has many hearts, and today plenty of Chinese families value girls as much as boys, but for millions of others—including my birth father—wanting a son is like believing in God: it is unquestionable. Limited by the one-child rule (a law that does not apply to the renegade republic of Taiwan), rural families in China still abandon, abort, and even kill their female offspring, even though Chinese leaders have outlawed ultrasounds and published propaganda promoting the value of girls. Mainland Chinese officials in 2007 predicted that the country would have an excess of fifteen million men by 2020, thanks to gender selection. The parents of thousands of little emperors soon will be forced to run around Asia begging and bargaining for brides. Even in modern Taiwan, divorce law still dictates that children belong to their father.

I had always known that one of the main reasons I had been given up was that I was a girl. It was always the most scandalous

part of the why-Mei-Ling-came-to-America lore. I thought—
thought—I understood it. I felt appropriately infuriated when I
read the books and heard the sayings: No sons, no happiness. A
family with only daughters is a dead end. Geese are more prof-
itable than girls. Girls are maggots in rice. I had seen fat baby
boys bounce on wedding beds and newlyweds drink lotus soup
and eat grapes to invoke male offspring. One such tradition even
slipped into my wedding ceremony in 2000, by accident. I asked
a Chinese American friend to find a traditional Chinese prayer
to read during our service. She could only find one that ended in
"a wish for many boys," which made my husband and me and
all our guests burst out in laughter.

I had every right to feel personally aggrieved by this belief,
but thanks to the careful nurturing of my American parents, I
thought I had risen above the whole Chinese male superiority
thing. It seemed almost inconsequential, a backward third-world
ideology that thrived in a place that I had escaped. I was now of
liberated and educated mind, and I could laugh at this idea and
discount it as a relic. It was part of my distant past, and I thought
that's where it would stay. It did not come to life for me until the
day I met my sisters.

MA AND BA had a boy in 1965, the Year of the Snake.
When they heard the baby's cries, they hoped their prayers had
been answered.

But once the child emerged, Ba, Ma, and Grandmother were
horrified. The boy's lip was bent up into a cleft. Euphoria disintegrated to despair. Some Chinese believe that if a pregnant
mother puts a sharp object such as a knife or scissors on her bed,
the child's lip in the womb may be cut. Ma believed that because
Ba made some changes in their house during her pregnancy and
knocked a hole in one wall, he had hurt the baby somehow.

The Chinese can be cruel to people who look or act differently. Even those who mean no harm are quick to ask about or point out your most negative traits, your fat stomach, your small, slanted eyes, or your dark skin. Not so long ago, the disfigured were outcasts, discriminated against and even beaten or killed. The intolerance continues today. As recently as the 1990s, Gansu Province had a law that called for the sterilization of people with hereditary deformities. In 2007 China declared that the country would not allow adoption of its orphans to foreigners who had "severe facial deformities." I'm often stunned at how often prejudice and superstition can overrule logic, love, and mercy.

In the 1960s surgery was available to correct cleft lips and palates and other birth defects in the modern world, but my family lived a different reality, one in which they could barely feed themselves. They could not imagine paying for the plastic surgery or the medical care that this boy might need. Within a few days of his birth, the boy died.

"He was sick," Ma and Ba would tell their daughters, relatives, and friends. Ma did not discuss the tragic details behind the child's death until many years later.

MY THIRD-OLDEST SISTER, Jin-Xia, was born in November of 1966, the Year of the Horse. The fourth, Jin-Hong, arrived in August 1968, the Year of the Monkey.

Ba and Grandmother were exasperated. He wanted to give his fourth daughter away; he tried to arrange a trade with another family, for a boy.

Grandmother said that they should keep her because she was flesh and blood. Jin-Hong stayed, but she got a special nickname, Awan, meaning "no more girls."

A fifth girl, Jin-Zhi was born in January 1971, the Year of the Dog, and Ba wanted to give her away, too, but Grandmother pointed out that the baby had a red rash on her head. A Chinese emperor long ago had the same kind of mark, and he became a highly successful leader.

"This child will be lucky for the family," Grandmother said.

Still, Ba believed that they could not afford another girl. He knew a tailor who wanted to adopt and took the baby to that man's home. Grandmother brought the child back.

"These are our children," she said. "They are our duty."

A gaggle of geese and no swans. The same destitution. The same life. My family worked from sunrise to sunset. Summers were fierce, and winters were harsh. They could hardly scrape the bare necessities from the soil. They still sold vegetables and tofu to soldiers and washed their clothing to earn extra coins. Then, in 1972, a man from Taiwan approached Ba.

He told them he had acres in Taitung. "You can live there, work in the fields, earn a better living, build a better life. Your family is big. You are barely able to feed your girls each day.

"Come to Taiwan," he said.

Ba agreed to scout Taitung to see what it was like. He traveled to Taiwan and stayed for three months in a small, lonely two-room hut in the fields of his new boss. The work was endless, but he could acquire land. The boss also promised to build Ba's family a several-room home.

I will bring my family here and our fortunes will be better, Ba thought. Despite having little more than a couple thousand Taiwan dollars in savings, he returned to Kinmen to move the family across the Taiwan Strait. They closed up their home, hoping to return better off one day. Standing before their shrine to Guanyin and the other gods, they held the bottom end of the burning incense with both hands and bowed their heads.

Please watch over us. Our fate is in your hands once again.

3

TWISTING FATE

On an army ship headed to Taiwan from Kinmen Island, August 1972

I imagine men in green khaki fatigues, armed and attentive, patrolling the immense deck. Soldiers and businessmen gather around makeshift tables, playing cards and drinking rice liquor. They are boozed up, cussing in Taiwanese and Mandarin, and laughing too loudly. Families, wary and tired, faces pale green with seasickness, huddle between luggage and giant crates.

My father is pacing, mingling with fellow passengers. He barely rests, even at night. He can't. He is too nervous, always anxious. The others try. Ma, a mother of five at twenty-nine years old, holds a baby to her breast.

This is her second trip to Taiwan. Last time it was her father dragging them across the sea, fleeing war. This time it is her husband who is searching for a new future. Ma is resigned to this move; it is beyond her power. She thinks only a little about their abrupt change in course and about what's behind and ahead. A moment between things.

Four girls ranging in age from nine to two run and play together in their small space on the deck floor. As the day stretches into night, the rolling sea is restless and passengers are vomiting. They also fear that China or Taiwan will mistakenly attack their boat. Most of my sisters sit on the floor and moan, trying not to think about throwing up. Jin-Hong, who is almost five with long braided hair and the only sister who is not sick, is excited by the adventure. She runs to the edge of the deck and looks out at the endless dark water rumbling beneath them, and it seems to go on forever and ever and ever. She thinks of falling through the empty air and the crash of the water around her, and her arms and legs flailing. She runs back to her family, suddenly frightened.

At some point, when all the play and the sickness has exhausted them, the girls curl up on the floor together near their mother and grandmother. Sweaty and small. Shoulders touching legs touching arms under heads on backs. Kicks, protests, tickles, giggles. Twitches and delicate snores. A pile of sisterhood.

After nearly twenty hours at sea, they see white sand and rocks rise up before them like the sun. The shore of Taiwan.

A Ilha Formosa. The Beautiful Island.

TAIWAN WAS BORN more than four million years ago, when the mammoth Eurasia and Philippine Sea tectonic plates collided. The seething earth rose like a serpent, and became the Central Mountain Range, the heart of the island, the source of the peaks and rivers that would fortify the land. In prehistoric times, Taiwan was connected by a land bridge to what would be Mainland China. The shifting earth and the rise and fall of the ocean caused the two land masses to crash and separate over and over, perhaps omen to their turbulent future relationship.

Since its frothy birth, Taiwan has been a constantly unquiet soul, a thrashing whale cradled by the Pacific Ocean and balanced precariously on the "rim of fire," the Asian continental shelf. Surrounded by the Pacific Ocean, the East and South China seas, the Luzon and the Taiwan straits, the Taiwan of today measures about 245 miles at its longest point and 90 miles at its widest. The Tropic of Cancer cuts the island through its middle; thus it straddles the Eastern and Northern hemispheres.

More than fifty fault lines zigzag across its face, throat, and belly, constantly pushing and heaving, folding and toppling, shaking and stirring the land. Those tremors have sculpted a tropical landscape that includes soaring limestone mountains, belligerent volcanoes, eerie valleys and basins, winding rivers and coral reefs, dramatic cliffs, rocky coastline, and terraced flatlands. Each year an average of four typhoons sweep across Taiwan. These storms and more frequent monsoons ply rice paddies and mangrove forests, as well as trigger deadly floods and mudslides. It was the island's mythical splendor (born of turbulence) that prompted Portuguese sailors in the 1500s to proclaim it *formosa,* which means "beautiful."

The dusty and tired Wang family arrived in Taitung, City of the East, in August of 1972, after enduring the long boat ride to the port city of Kaohsiung, and then a meandering five-hour bus ride, sea to sea, traversing miles of rice paddies and the mountains.

The town that welcomed them was barely a spot on the map, with the sierras at its back and the Pacific Ocean foaming at its feet. The gray sand and rock coastline of Taitung county is almost 144 miles long, but few people lived there, thanks to its penchant for typhoons and earthquakes. The Chinese did not establish themselves in the region until the late nineteenth century, and even by the 1970s few Mandarin-speaking Nationalist Chinese had made their way south to Taitung. Most people spoke Holo or the languages of aboriginal tribes such as the Atayal, Saisiyat, Paiwan, Rukai, Puyuma, Thao, and Yami.

Taitung was a sprinkling of government buildings, shops, and a Catholic hospital called St. Mary's. Local officials had built one train station, an overly optimistic project that they hoped would connect the region with the rest of Taiwan and create an economic boom. Few roads were paved. In America, men in bell-bottomed pants were wooing ladies with flipped hair and liquid eyeliner and parking their Ford Mustangs in suburban garages. In Taitung, autos were a luxury. Almost everyone walked or rode bikes, hoisting their wares on their shoulders or on the backs of water buffalo.

Mostly, there was land. Miles and miles of rice paddies, corn-stalks, and soybeans to be watered and picked. The sweaty future of my family stretched out in shades of brown and green.

They stayed in a cramped hut until their patron built them a house, a solid structure of steel and concrete, with a living room, dining room, kitchen, four bedrooms, two bathrooms, and a courtyard where Ma could wash and hang clothes and keep a garden. No more sleeping one atop the other. I bet my sisters were ecstatic, running through the house, their bare feet slapping on the cold tile, their shrieks echoing through the halls. They might have installed themselves in the rooms they wanted and bickered with each other over who would sleep where. On the top floor, Ma and Ba re-created their ancestral shrine and hung a picture of Ba's father on the wall.

Our family was still dirt poor. Each month they earned about twenty-five hundred Taiwan dollars, or the equivalent of less than sixty-five U.S. dollars. Every day Ma and Ba dedicated themselves to working their patron's land, digging in the dirt, baking in the sun, raising rice, corn, sweet potato, and eggplant.

My sisters were becoming a handsome group, with shiny hair and round faces. They were all bright and strong-willed like our father, but each girl was developing her own distinct personality. On the eve of 1973, the oldest, Jin-Feng, was ten. She was *dajie*, big sister, and acted like it, tough and knowing. Because of her age, she would be forced to spend more of her time in the field with our parents, but she would be the first woman in our family to graduate from high school and later college. Jin-Qiong, sister no. 2, was the most gentle in nature of all the sisters, caring and unusually patient. She was the most forgiving of her family's faults, always fussing over her sisters, buying them things, covering for their bad behavior.

Third sister, Jin-Xia, was almost a carbon copy of Ba: strong and passionate. She was his favorite as a child. If she had a cough, he excused her from housework. He fawned over her and she adored him, though she developed his temper. Arguments between the two would become legendary, characterized by high-pitched yelling and the occasional object hurled through the air. Jin-Hong, sister no. 4, was pretty, smart, and responsible as a child. She was popular with friends and boys and became a phenomenal cook. The fifth, Jin-Zhi, was still a baby, chubby and happy. She would grow into a class clown, funny, but especially sensitive to our mother's plight and our father's manic behavior.

When they were old enough, the girls were recruited to help their parents work. At 6 a.m. their wake-up call would fill the house.

Get up! Grandmother would shriek. *Get up!*

If her shrill voice failed to rouse them, if my sisters lingered for too long in the sleepy haze of childhood, they would feel a sharp yank on their ear or a digging pinch to their thigh or arm that snatched them violently from their dreams. They would screech in protest, wiping tears from their eyes and would sit up, not wanting to be scolded again. They pulled on their clothes and trudged the thirty-minute walk to Beinan School. On the weekends, they worked in the fields with their parents. Each specialized in a different task, picking rocks out of the soil, planting seeds, or pulling weeds.

I had a cushy childhood in comparison. Each morning my parents woke me up by gently opening my bedroom door and calling to me, "Rise and shine, sleepyhead!" My dad poured milk in my cereal or carefully sliced a half grapefruit so I could easily spoon out the tiny triangles of pulp with a serrated-tip spoon. My mom braided or curled my hair while I would sing. A yellow bus picked me up and drove me barely two miles to Holland Elementary School. After school, I had Brownies or T-ball or some other fun activity. Later, I would spread my homework on our round kitchen table and then draw, read, write, or play until I went to bed.

For my sisters, there were no after-school activities. The girls walked home from school, set down their schoolbags, and cleaned, swept, and washed or did their homework. The only way they could get out of their chores was if they had a test the next day.

TAIWAN GAVE THE WANGS a son but not in the way my parents had expected or hoped.

Shortly after they arrived, they met a couple from the south-central city of Chiayi who were even poorer than they were and could not feed their only son. They were afraid the boy would die from hunger and offered their child to Ba and Ma.

My parents could not afford more children; they could barely support the girls they had. Each time a girl had been born in recent years, they had considered giving her away, but this was different. This boy could be the One—or act as a backup until another One was born. Ba and Ma took the baby into their home, named him Nian-Zu, and he became their chosen son.

They did this in secret. In Taiwan the inability to have children is considered humiliating for many families and adoption is thought of as a last option for the infertile. Likewise, the idea that parents would give away their precious children—boys or girls—is embarrassing. In 2005, according to the Child Welfare League Foundation of the Republic of China, only 10 percent of approximately five thousand abandoned children could find homes, and officials blamed prejudice against adoption. Many of the adoptions that do exist are private arrangements, father to brother, mother to sister, friend to friend. Many adopted children are never told they are adopted, and Ba and Ma would never tell their son that his "real" parents gave him up, even if everyone else in his family knew. They would not want him to feel bad about himself.

Our parents and grandmother obviously favored Nian-Zu, my sisters recalled. He was handsome, with a tussle of dark hair and a sweet and mischievous smile. Grandmother, who took care of the children while our parents worked, gave Nian-Zu an extra egg or piece of meat. My parents fawned over his every coo and need. Ma was pregnant again—with me this time—but her attention was focused squarely on her boy.

The Wangs would pour their hopes into their son, unaware that he would not complete them.

MA GAVE BIRTH to me in the Year of the Ox, the Chinese year of 4670–4671, on August 26, 1973. She cried out in pain as a fierce labor consumed her, frightening my sisters. Ba rushed her to St. Mary's Hospital.

I was born a Water Ox. Another girl.

My parents had just adopted a boy, and they had five girls already.

"We cannot afford another," Ba said once again. He asked the nurses if they knew of anyone who might want to adopt me.

A pretty, young American nun happened to be working as a midwife in the hospital. Sister Maureen Sinnott had been corresponding with a couple in America who wanted to adopt a child. The meeting seemed fortuitous. She told Ma and Ba about the couple.

"They are good people," she said, "and they are well equipped to educate, love, and care for your baby."

Ma did not want to give up her daughter. She wondered: *How do we know that she would go to a good place, to a good family? How could we send this child so far away, so far from her flesh and blood? Is it not our obligation as parents to care for her?*

Ba said, "She has the chance for something better."

"Then why couldn't we give the baby to a family in Taiwan?" At least she would be able to visit her daughter. At least she would be able to see that her child was okay and not lost somewhere in a country she could never visit, could not even imagine.

"What kind of Chinese family would want to adopt a girl?" Ba said.

He asked Sister Maureen, "Are these people good?"

The nun assured him, "Yes, and they will love your daughter."

Despite her doubts, Ma deferred to Ba's resolute judgment, ever the dutiful wife and mother. She had not been able to give the Wangs a blood-born son, so what right did she have to complain? It was decided. The sixth daughter would go to America. The nun gathered me into her arms and took me away.

"Do you want to receive the medicine, the injection to dry up your breast milk, now that you will not have to nurse your daughter?" Sister Maureen asked Ma.

"No," Ma said, "I have a one-year-old son I can feed."

Maureen noted her response in my medical charts.

Ma went home and I stayed in the care of the hospital staff. The nurses named me Mei-Ling, Sister Maureen's Chinese name, breaking the family tradition of naming daughters after Kinmen Island. I grew fat and happy, lugged around on the backs of nurses and in the arms of nuns, and my laughter and cries filled the hospital corridors.

Ba visited the hospital occasionally to bring the priest, nuns, and nurses gifts of appreciation, such as a live chicken. Ma would not go because she could not bear to be reminded of what they had done.

She had hoped that I would leave as soon as possible, but the brutal bureaucracies of both Taiwan and United States prolonged the adoption process. Ba and Ma had to appear in court with the nun to sign any necessary paperwork and to assure the Taiwan judges that this was what they wanted.

Ma did not see me again until the day I left Taitung for good in April 1974. The whole family came to the hospital to say good-bye: Ma, Ba, Grandmother, aunties, and daughters. Ma was pregnant, her belly rising into familiar curves. She and Ba were hoping, once again, for a boy. The nuns and nurses chattered like swallows, flitting about in front of the hospital as they assembled to take photos. Cameras in that time and place were somewhat of a novelty and the Chinese loved to be photographed. Everyone was teary, too, because they all had had some part in caring for me.

Sister Maureen had grown attached to me. She held me close in every photo, even the ones that included my relatives. I probably would not have even known my birth mother from the dozens of warm bodies who had acted as my surrogate parents during those months after my birth, so when it was time for Ma to pose for the cameras, she did not try to hold me or assume for a minute the role that she had given away. She did not believe that it was her place to change the course of events, as much as she might have longed to. A pact had been made and the papers were signed. To turn back now would mean losing face, something Ba would not risk. I belonged to another mother, another father, another destiny. Ma could only hope this was the right decision.

"Move closer together. Smile for the camera."

She tried her best. Ma stood next to the nun, squinted in the springtime sunshine and forced a faint smile to her lips. She reached out and touched her fidgeting baby's arm. It was the best she could do. Maybe I might see this photo one day and sense the apology that shuddered in the depth of her heart.

4

THE ODD COUPLE

Taylor, Michigan, 1972

Rollie Hopgood was not Chris's type. At all.

She knew him through the small universe of teachers in Taylor, Michigan, where she had recently taken a job. Who didn't know Hopgood? Rollie was a bald, bushy-bearded art teacher and well-known union leader in the blue-collar Detroit suburb. He led the union meetings, and he told everyone what to do and how to do it. You either adored him or despised him, depending on the side you were on. You definitely could never forget him once you met him, or heard him. He filled rooms with his presence and his opinions. On the picket line, he rarely needed a megaphone, thanks to his booming voice.

Diane Christner—nicknamed Chris by friends and family—was a quiet blonde, thoughtful and meticulous, who had grown up in a suburb of Flint. Chris had accepted a job as an elementary school teacher in Taylor just before her first marriage failed.

She and Rollie were paired together during a bowling outing. The players with the higher bowling averages were paired with those with lower scores; Rollie had bowled a perfect 300 before; Chris averaged around 150. He was divorced, too, and seemed interested in her. He complimented her game and hinted that they should go out sometime. She tried to change the subject; his boldness intimidated her.

A friend slipped Rollie her phone number. He called, and the two talked for almost two hours. He convinced her to go out with him. She was single now, a bit bored and lonely. Why not?

He showed up on the steps of her Southgate apartment wearing stylish red plaid pants and shiny black shoes and carrying flowers. He arrived in a blue Porsche, and told her that he thought they could go to Northville Downs, a nearby horseracing track. Chris had never bet on horses before.

"Sounds fun," she said.

To her pleasant surprise, Hopgood was not slick. He did not drive or talk fast. He politely held open the car door. He patiently taught her how to place a bet on a horse and gave her money to place those bets. He spoke passionately about the things he loved: teaching, his students, the union movement, baseball. They discussed their profession and all the people they knew in common. Chris's ex-husband had been a scientist, a brain, and she always felt silly talking about her career with him. Rollie loved what they did for a living. His enthusiasm and good humor charmed her. Joy spread like sunlight, lighting up his blue eyes and opening a wide, toothy grin, silver-filled molars and all. He had a laugh like a whip.

They talked about everything. He told her about his childhood in Taylor, she mentioned her family in Burton, Michigan. He attended Western Michigan University, where he briefly pitched on the baseball team; she attended Adrian College. They both said they wanted children and were ready now. They gabbed all night and did not realize the sun had risen until the paperboy came to her door.

Chris had never been out with a man like Rollie before, so attentive and compassionate. He made her feel safe, like he would take care of everything she needed before she knew what she needed. She was quiet and he was loud. He thrived on attention; she liked her privacy. They were yin and yang, but they seemed to fit just right. She knew immediately, when she felt the pounding of her heart, the lightening of limbs and head, that she had fallen in love. It was a connection she had never made before. He seemed smitten as well. Surely, he would call the next day. Surely.

But Saturday passed and Sunday passed. And then Monday. Chris was shocked.

Play it cool, she thought. When he did call on about Wednesday, she acted like the minutes had not crept by.

Rollie asked her out again and she agreed. They met for dinner, and he explained that he had gone out with three different women he had been seeing casually, one each night. He told her that he needed to break the news to all of them. He told them that he had met the One.

Chris was the One.

They had seemed an unlikely pair, but immediately they were inseparable. Rollie moved into Chris's apartment within days. Three weeks after they met, on a Friday, September 15, 1972, they invited two friends out to lunch in downtown Detroit. Motown continued to smart from the race riots of 1967, but Rollie still loved the city. They met in the City-County Building on Woodward Avenue, where sharply dressed lawyers and politicians rushed in and out of heavy doors. Chris wore a beige suit, with a short jacket and a skirt that cut above the knee and complimented her shapely legs. In the lobby, Chris and Rollie announced to their pals that they were getting married and they wanted them to be witnesses.

Are we insane? Chris asked herself as she stole a second for herself in a quiet corridor before the ceremony. She was not impulsive, but she was thirty and he was thirty-two. They had both suffered the trauma of failed marriages at a time when divorce was neither common nor socially accepted. They knew what they wanted. They wanted each other and they wanted a family, and they weren't going to go about it in the conventional way.

She straightened her suit, and she and Rollie took their place in a queue of couples. They stood before a judge and repeated the generic oaths, though they made sure that neither of them had to say the word *obey*. The judge pronounced them husband and wife; they kissed and went out to lunch to celebrate.

That evening, the newlyweds crossed the Ambassador Bridge into Windsor, Ontario, for an international wedding night. They called their parents from a Holiday Inn room that overlooked the Detroit River.

"Guess what?" Rollie told his mother. "I'm lying next to the most beautiful woman in the world. And she's my wife." The Taylor School District was abuzz with the gossip that the uproarious Rollie Hopgood had married the composed Diane Christner. *Did you even know they were dating? They are sooo different! How could this possibly work?*

The couple drove home on Sunday, stopping in Pontiac to attend a Detroit Lions football game. They each wore the wedding rings that Rollie had designed and made at a Dearborn jewelry shop, yellow gold on a black background, straight, narrow lines with circles on the ends, each nestled perfectly against the other.

ROLLIE HAD PROBLEMS having children with his first wife and had a hunch that he was sterile. Tests confirmed his suspicions, so he and Chris began to inquire about adoption. Yet, in the eyes of the many adoption agencies at the time, the couple had an endless number of strikes against them: They were both teachers, and Chris was not willing to quit working. They were older and both had been divorced. Plus, they did not practice a religion, which some adoption agencies considered a problem. Chris's family had never been particularly religious when she was young, although they did attend church regularly. Rollie rejected organized religion after he almost died in a horrible car accident when he was about twenty. He was in the backseat of a car that was hurling way too fast down a city street when another car struck his. He wasn't wearing a seat belt and crashed through the windshield, nearly splitting his skull. His minister came to his bedside in the hospital and told him he was being punished for not attending church that weekend. Rollie never went back.

My parents' prospects did not look good. Then a friend who worked in the school district told them about her sister-in-law, Maureen Sinnott, a nun who worked as a midwife in rural Taiwan.

Chris and Rollie wrote to Maureen, introducing themselves politely and directly: "We want a child, and we hope you can help."

ALMOST EVERYONE WANTS to be a nun at some point, at least that's what Maureen Sinnott once thought. Religion was an essential part of her childhood in Allen Park. Her parents prayed with a black rosary every night before going to bed, said grace before every meal, and attended church at least once a week. Maureen deeply admired the nuns at St. Frances Cabrini Grade School and St. Francis Xavier High School. When she was in eighth grade, she even asked her parents if she could become a nun.

"Not yet," they said.

Maureen asked again when she graduated from high school.

"Why don't you get a professional degree first," suggested her parents, who were not opposed but wanted her to think hard about such a big decision. Maureen started to date a nice man. He wanted to marry her. She loved him but knew she had to try her dream, to follow that part of her heart to see where it led.

In 1960, at eighteen years old, she took her first plane ride ever to Boston to join the Medical Missionaries of Mary, an Irish order of nuns. She liked the order because their hair showed beneath their veils and they wore slightly shorter skirts than in other orders, just below knee length. They seemed more feminine, more like her. She studied there for three years and professed in 1963. She then went on to nursing school and later Ireland to study midwifery. She loved this world of intimacy with God, of sisterhood. She was wide-eyed and full of hope that she could do good in the world. She wanted to go to Africa because she had seen movies about missionaries who saved people in the bush. Later in life, she would turn against going to foreign countries with the goal of converting the natives, but at that time she believed spreading the word of God was the most meaningful thing she could do.

In 1967 the Superiors asked if she would go to Formosa.

Where is that? she thought. She went to the library and read about this place off the coast of China, known to the Western World as Formosa and to its inhabitants as Taiwan, which means "the terraced bay" in Chinese. Taiwan was completely new and seemed exciting.

"I'll go," she said. At twenty-six years old, she flew west, to California, Seattle, and then Taiwan. She spent two years in the city of Hsinchu, where she studied Mandarin with other nuns and priests. They sat in a small classroom almost every day, all day, reading, writing, reciting. "*Wo . . . Ni . . . Ta . . .*"

In 1969 Maureen began her time as a midwife in southern Taiwan. She took the train to Kaohsiung from Taipei and then the bus to Taitung. She was enchanted by the simplicity of the town back then: the palm trees; the bald Buddist nuns on their old bicycles; the short, one-story buildings, except for St. Mary's Hospital, which had two levels. She lived with three Irish nuns on the second floor of the convent next to St. Mary's. The dozen or so local nurses lived beneath them in cramped quarters on the first floor. From the convent, she could see a Chinese temple. During the mornings, farmers hauled buckets of manure on bamboo poles laid across their shoulders. The nuns and nurses ate vegetables and rice for most meals and sometimes fish on special days. They didn't have luxuries such as sugar, sweets, or milk for their morning coffee, but Maureen loved this bare-bones existence.

Many of the mothers who came to the hospital were poor women who had been matched through arranged marriages. They often were very young girls with old husbands. Maureen and the nuns took turns staying up at night, attending to patients and babies. At St. Mary's, the midwives were expected to do procedures that they might not in other places, such as delivering twins and handling cases of placenta previa, in which a low-lying placenta endangers the health of the mother and fetus. Resources and help were short, so everyone pitched in.

At first, Maureen struggled with Mandarin. For example, for a long time she thought she was asking women who did not plan to breast-feed: "Would you like your breast milk dried up?" The women stared blankly at her. Weeks after she had been repeating this phrase over and over, the nurses and the patient broke into a shy giggle.

"Why are you laughing?" Maureen asked.

"Because you are asking us if our cow's milk is dried up."

Maureen had worked at the hospital for about three years when her sister-in-law in Michigan wrote to her to tell her about two friends, Rollie and Chris Hopgood, who wanted to adopt a baby.

"Maybe you could help them," she suggested.

Sometimes babies, especially girls, were abandoned at the hospital. Not often, but once in a while. It was not something Maureen normally did; she was swamped with work and patients at the hospital, and it would take considerable perseverance and time to pull this off.

I will do it, she decided, unaware of just how tough it would be.

. . .

May 15, 1973
Dear Mr. and Mrs. Hopgood,

Thank you very much for your letter and I want to assure you that I will do everything possible to help you. Unfortunately the agency that had given me such hope now tells me that it is the policy of Taiwan to completely resist adoptions to foreigners at the present time. He said that in the future it will be possible again. Please do not get too downhearted because I still plan to contact other agencies . . . It would mean a lot to me if I could help you to adopt a Chinese baby because I am so in love with the Chinese people and their culture that I want to share this love with everyone. I know life would be so much more meaningful for you if you had a baby . . . Keep optimistic—if possible. I will do my very best to help you.
Love, Sr. Maureen

July 9, 1973
Dear Mr. and Mrs. Hopgood,

It has been a while since I wrote to you because until now I have not had any news. But on my way up to meet Danny [Maureen's brother], I stopped at a convent. They said that they have a baby for adoption, a one month old girl who was abandoned on a train so she has no known parents which means that the adoption procedure would be very simple and you could have her within 1 or 2 months. The only problem is that she has a lip/cleft palate but with surgery she could look normal. Nowadays this type of surgery is commonplace. If you are doubtful as to what harelip/cleft palate means, you could ask your doctor. I would advise you to adopt this baby because there seems to be very few babies available, and because her parents abandoned her the adoption procedure will not involve all the red tape in ordinary cases. I am going to see the baby in Taipei Monday and then I will await your answer . . . I think it would be beautiful to give love to a little girl who was abandoned but this must be your own decision . . . Love, Reen

Rollie and Chris wrote back that they could take the child but then received this letter:

August 20, 1973
Dear Mr. and Mrs. Hopgood,

Yesterday a baby girl was born in our hospital (perfectly normal) and the 21 year old mother wants to give her away. The reason: because the father of the child was already married but he didn't tell this woman until she was already pregnant. They have already (she and her mother—the mother's permission is very important in Chinese society) agreed to give you the baby if you want her. So now I must ask you if you are willing to accept an illegitimate baby? To tell the truth, I think that would be the only kind of a child that the parents would be willing to let go to the U.S. Please talk it over and then let me know what you decide as soon as possible. Love, Maureen

Chris and Rollie again were willing to take the child. However, this postcard arrived ten days later:

August 30, 1973
Quite a few of our [letters] from here have gone astray lately so I am writing twice to tell you about the beautiful baby I have for you. Since I wrote you the letter last week I have another one—much more beautiful and legitimate. So I am looking forward to hearing from you as soon as possible. She is tiny and has long black hair. I'm in love with her. Her parents already have 5 girls and cannot afford to raise another. Her 5 sisters are very pretty. Love, Sr. Maureen

The Hopgoods told Maureen to proceed with the adoption.

Maureen advised that my parents come to Taiwan with a letter from the police saying they were good citizens and with financial records showing that they could support the child. She told them they might have to appear in court with the birth parents. On September 28, 1973, she wrote:

They are a beautiful couple and I know that you will love them. They have never mentioned money to me but it is a Chinese custom that the adopting parents would give $75–100 American dollars. The court fees should not exceed $100.
Did you receive the photos of your new baby? She is much more beautiful than the photos!! I am anxiously awaiting your arrival . . . God Bless you, Maureen

October 4, 1973
Dear Mr. and Mrs. Hopgood,
Today I received this very disappointing letter from Fr. O'Neill who is in charge of Catholic Relief Services and has a lot of ex-

*perience helping people adopt babies. But please don't be too
disappointed because with God's help we will find a way. My
purpose in writing you is just to tell you [you] had better wait in
making definite plans about coming to Taiwan. Please forgive
me because I know that I have caused you so much trouble in
already writing to tell you to prepare.*

In a letter to Maureen, dated October 4, 1973, Francis O'Neill,
director of Catholic Relief Services in Taipei, Taiwan, wrote:

*I am afraid you are going to run into difficulties in the case that
you are handling for your friend. The child has both natural
parents still alive and they are willing to go to court with you
which is very good but I do not think you understand that the
American consulate here has a regulation for the child whose
natural parents are still alive. The Chinese legal procedure is very
simple but the U.S. Consulate requires that such a child remain
in the country of its origin for one or maybe two years before
they will issue a visa for the child to go to America. The reason
for this I am told is that the U.S. people must be assured there
will no "kick back" from natural parents . . . Sincerely yours,
Francis K. O'Neill*

Maureen remained upbeat when writing to Chris and Rollie:

*I have written so many letters to so many agencies and re-
ceived so many contradicting replies that it is hard to know what
to do. But all that I know is that little "May Ling" will be yours
soon if you are patient and persevering. By the way do you belong to any religious sect? That does not influence me in any way
about the baby but if I know that you believe in God I could at
least ask you to pray. Love, Sr. Maureen*

October 21, 1973

Dear Diane and Rollie,

I received your long letter and was relieved that you understand so well that it will be a little slow-going. But if we are patient and at the same time do everything in our power—I know that you will have the little May Ling in your arms in the next few months ... Father (Peter) Cheng [a priest at St. Mary's] and I went to the law court to see if we could adopt the baby for you by proxy. (This is really very funny, you know—a priest and a nun in the adoption court—smile!) The lawyers said that they would do everything to help us (their wives had babies in the hospital) ... Yes, May Ling lives in the hospital with us so I am within crying distance almost 24 hours a day. Our nurses are continuously hugging and loving her so she certainly will not be lacking. I feel myself so attached to her that I want to hurry the procedure along before she gets to recognize people. You asked what would happen to her if law prohibits her from going to the U.S. There are many Chinese couples unable to have children who would adopt her. But let's be optimistic and believe she will be yours soon. You asked me if we needed money to cover the details and caring for baby. At this time everything is fine. Don't worry about anything like that, ok?

On November 3, 1973, Maureen sent an English translation of a Chinese form that mistakenly identified me as "Yang, Mei-Ling," using my mother's surname instead of that of my father. I would believe Yang was my biological surname until I received the first letter from my birth family in 1997.

November 5, 1973

Just after mailing you the letter yesterday ... I received your letter saying you are personal friends with your Congressman

[William Ford]. By all means go to him and ask him to help you. As I said before the procedure for adopting the baby for you in Taiwan is as simple as it can be. The problem is only on the American side. We need big shots in the American government to help us ... Love, Maureen.

A November 9 letter from John D. Barfield, consul in the U.S. embassy in Taiwan, to Maureen explained that the adopted alien child of U.S. citizens would not be given any preferential status to facilitate the child's immigration, except in the case of an orphan.

A November 14, 1973, letter to Sister Maureen from Father Francis McGrath in Taipei, who was helping Maureen, noted that a conversation with a district director of U.S. immigration services was "not cheering." U.S. law provided for an expedited process only in the case of needy children, like those whose parents had died.

I am sorry about this sister. At the best of times, with people living here who wish to adopt a baby, it is a painful and anxious business. From the start I felt that your case was somewhat unusual and that there would be problems. From the point of view of the parents who wish to have their baby girl adopted, it should be possible to find good Chinese parents here. It is not uncommon today for childless Chinese to adopt children ... It's too bad after all your trouble that the situation should prove to be as it seems to be ... With kindest regards to all the Sisters. God Bless.

Fifteen days later, word came to Chris and Rollie from William E. Zimmer, assistant director of travel control for the U.S. Department of Justice, that my visa application was being processed.

Two days after Christmas Maureen wrote that an interview with the U.S. embassy in Taipei was scheduled on January 7, 1974. She said that my birth parents would like a picture of my new parents with me.

Yesterday we [Father Cheng and I] went to the court and adopted the baby for you. It took 7 hours to do because every-thing in English had to be translated into Chinese and everything in Chinese had to be translated into English . . . Yang Mei Ling is legally your baby. We begged them to give us a statement that the child was abandoned but according to Taiwanese law, they cannot so we must hope for the best with the documents we have . . .

The parents are really good people—just unable to support her. I have come to know and love them. They have gone to court with me at least 7 times on false alarms where we were told we needed some other document, etc. and they never said a word. Unfortunately a reporter was at the court yesterday and wrote a big article in the daily newspaper about the adoption. We begged him not to because the parents "lose face."

January 1974
Mei Ling and I and one of our nurses left Taitung Jan. 6 at 8 a.m. by train to Hualian then flew to Taipei. We stayed over-night in a small room with one of our former nurses and Mei Ling was very good, only crying for her midnight and 4 a.m. feed. On Mon. we went to the American Embassy for our ap-pointment and I was quite disappointed. The Vice Consul only asked me about three questions about Mei Ling's health, fam-ily, etc.—simple questions that could have been answered by mail . . . Then she told us to go to the Chinese Embassy to get her passport but they would not give it to us because we lacked

some documents. I asked the Vice Consul if it would be safe to buy Mei Ling's plane ticket for late February and she said it is too uncertain so we must keep praying. It seems that every time we think we are almost there something new pops up.

I really learned what it was like to be a mother while I was in Taipei, washing diapers, preparing bottles, walking her to sleep. But the more I do for her, the more I love her. She does not recognize me yet, but is very close to it, probably in another 2–3 weeks. She laughs out loud now and is able to almost turn over from her tummy. I am sorry that you are missing all of these "firsts" of hers. She weighs almost 14 pounds and her legs and arms are beautiful and strong due to the Enfamil milk, which is the best. She stands very straight on her legs when you hold her up by her hands. She has a temper too, especially when she is hungry and she drools saliva constantly so we always have a bib on her. We bought all new clothes and she looks beautiful in them. I bought several Chinese suits because I thought you would like them, but probably she will have outgrown them by the time you see her . . . Maureen.

February 8, 1974
Dear Diane and Rollie,

It was wonderful to talk with you on the phone and I could not believe how clear your voices sounded . . . we are still working on the passport here. We cannot buy the air tickets until we have the American visa and Chinese passport so I doubt if she will be with you before early March. She has had a little cold the past few days but she'll be all right. She has been rolling over from her stomach to her back. She rarely lays on her stomach. The Chinese always keep their babies on their back. She eats watery rice off our chopsticks and mashed carrots. We cannot buy baby food in this part of Taiwan. During Chinese

New Year prices went up on rice, clothes, food, gas, etc. 100%. This was not a gradual up rise so it is rather a shock for people. Airfare, bus fare, etc. all doubled and we heard it will increase in Spring.

Mei Ling does not have any teeth yet (it's too early) but she puts everything she can get her hands on into her mouth, especially her fingers. When she is tired she rubs her eyes and cries which means she wants to sleep. She is especially beautiful when she wakes up from her naps—her cheeks are rosy and she smiles and smiles. She laughs out loud if you tickle her and her body is beautiful, strong and fat. She loves to be bathed. She drools so much that we have to keep powder under her double chin to prevent chafing. She talks baby talk. I have a habit of saying Ohhhh to her and she repeats. She is beginning to imitate. Unfortunately one of the nurses taught her how to stick her tongue out. (Smile).

I loved your letter of Jan. 20 with your photos and so much information about yourselves. After I read that I felt I really knew you and love you. I think it is beautiful that you are going to keep Mei Ling's name (pronounced May Ling). I'm so happy you both love sports, and especially I'm happy you will be teaching Mei Ling to swim. Her dad comes now and then. At one point he told me that it is their custom for you to buy them a few clothes so I will buy them here when I go to Taipei. Speaking of money, I have talked it over with the other sisters and we feel that $2,000 U.S. will cover everything from beginning to end. Of course, it includes the airplane tickets to Michigan . . . I assure you the money doesn't mean a thing to me or the other sisters—it is only to pay for her milk, clothes, court, travel expenses. It's great your mom [Chris's mother] works in a baby store. I'm sure she's picking out clothes for Mei Ling. She is a very lucky baby because I know that your hearts already love her as

much as we do, and will gradually love her even more. You can-
not know how sad my heart will be the day I say good-bye to her
at the airport. I only know that the sooner she is in your arms the
better it is for all of us. Separation is painful . . . Love, Maureen

On February 26, 1974, Congressman William D. Ford wrote to my parents to tell them his staff has asked officials in the Taiwan embassy in the United States help expedite the adoption process.

March 2, 1974
Dear Rollie and Chris,
 Today I received your check for $2,000 U.S. If we find it is
too much I will send the extra back with Mei Ling. Much of it
will be used for "favors" which is customary in Chinese society.
For instance, we will have to give a little "gift" to the man in the
court working towards her passport. Getting the Chinese pass-
port has been much more difficult than expected. In Taipei they
insist on the official, original documents that you sent giving
Fr. Cheng and me the authority to adopt for you. But the court
in Taitung refuses to release anything but photo static copies
because all her papers have been bound and sealed and are not
allowed to be tampered with or separated. These are the unex-
pected problems that we are still working on. But I know a man
who knows how to buy these kind of favors and that seems to be
the only way to get Mei Ling moving. I decided we should take a
six month photograph in her red Chinese suit to send you in case
there is a delay of a few more weeks. At least you will see how
she has grown in the past 2 months . . . She has been sheltered
a bit too much which I noticed when I take her out to a strange
place she gets afraid so I am trying to make a real effort to let her
experience strange situations because I'm afraid she will find the

travel to America too strange and cry, etc. I can't tell you what she means to me. I have never taken care of a baby for 6 months and I just know that I love her so much.

Can you believe that we have almost completed all this? God is good and everyone here has been praying that she would soon be yours. Many of the people working in adoptions here cannot believe that we succeeded so soon (smile). You have been waiting a long time—she will be everything that you are longing for and more. May she complete your marriage. All my love, Maureen

P.S. I kiss Mei Ling at least 100 time a day so some are from you!

March 14, 1974

This letter does not bring much news but I know that you like to hear as often as possible how your princess daughter is progressing. She continues to say "baba" and still no sign of teeth but wears a constant smile and is outgrowing her clothes rapidly. She has quite a tummy . . . She is beginning to recognize people. There is one man who has a beard and when she was younger he used to rub her smooth skin against his rough beard and although he was teasing she didn't like it. Now if he comes within 10 feet of her, she cries . . . No, Mei Ling is not baptized. We would only baptize her if you were both Catholic. But of course my big desire will always be that she will sometime find God and be baptized. That is my prayer for her. Of course, I will pray for her safe trip, too . . . Diane, you sound so excited that you are having difficulty sleeping. It makes me so happy to hear how much you love her already and I read and re-read your letter about her red, white, and blue room. The sisters and nurses have been following every detail because she is so much a part of all of us. It makes us so happy to hear how you have prepared for her—even her Easter dress! . . . Tell me every detail when she

*arrives with you and my last request will be that you telegram
me when you have her in your arms so I can feel at peace . . . I
feel so close to both of you—we are friends in every sense of the
word. (P.S. You can call me Maureen. It's more friendly than
S.M.— Sister Maureen. Mei Ling is 17 pounds, 12 oz.)*

March 25, 1974
Dear Rollie and Chris:
    *Today I received her passport from the Taiwan government.
So I immediately phoned long distance to Amer. Embassy in
Taipei for an appointment . . . Her father came to visit her
today—she wouldn't go to him at first but then she let him hold
her. She is getting to know us and she is afraid of very dark
skinned Chinese people (so you two are safe!) I still think it
would help Mei Ling a lot to adjust to you if you wear a white
blouse or shirt when you pick her up at the airport. Once you
get her home and she is used to you (after about 1 hour) it won't
matter what you wear. She is so lovable—we just want to make
her adjustment as natural as possible. You must be so excited!*

    On April 7, 1974, all the nurses and my birth family gathered
to take pictures and say good-bye before our train left Taitung
at 8 a.m. More nuns and a priest met us in the city of Hualian
and drove us on the back of their motorcycles to the convent
for dinner before we headed to the Hualian airport. The roar
of the airplanes scared me, Maureen recalled. I never cried but
my eyes were as big as saucers. We arrived in Taipei that night,
and Maureen searched for a hotel. She found a cheap little place
downtown, and we settled into our tiny room. She was exhausted
and didn't realize the kind of hotel she had chosen—until she
saw all the American GIs and their "girlfriends."
    Oh my, she thought. *We must be such a sight! A young Ameri-*

can nun in her veil with a Chinese baby in arms wandering the
halls of this seedy place . . .

The next day, someone broke into the room and stole her passport, a couple thousand Taiwan dollars, and several pictures. The
thief, a boy, returned soon after and gave back the passport, apol-
ogizing profusely, fearing that he might be punished for swiping
a foreigner's documents. Meanwhile, the bureaucratic nightmare
continued. Many of my American papers identified me improp-
erly as Yang Mei-Ling and all of my Chinese documents referred
to me as Wang Mei-Ling. There also was a two-hour wait for the
required physical exam. Once all that was done, officials at the
U.S. embassy told Maureen that I was missing a document, but
then they generously overlooked the omission.

During those final nights, Maureen wrote instructions to my
parents, describing my schedule in detail to help make the transi-
tion easier.

"She will probably take a while to settle down. It is unfortu-
nate that she did not get to America 1 month ago because now
she recognizes all of us. She will not go to strangers. She cries—
especially if men try to hold her (that will change in a few years—
smile). She probably won't like Rollie's mustache but she will get
used to it."

CHRIS AND ROLLIE arrived in San Francisco the second
week of April, all prepared to receive me the next morning. *Finally!* They spent the night in the airport Holiday Inn, barely able
to sleep. They were just leaving the hotel when the phone rang. It
was Maureen.

"Japan Airlines has gone on strike," she told them. More than
seven million workers had called a general strike in Japan. They
boycotted airlines, railroads, subways, buses, taxis, and shipping
lines. They left their posts in schools, post offices, telegraph and

government offices. The Japanese mint stopped printing money and the rangers in national forests refused to take their posts. They wanted a pay hike of 30 percent to match the skyrocketing inflation caused by oil prices. Tokyo's banks and office buildings turned into sleeping quarters because employees had no way to get home. Japan Airlines had to cancel sixteen of its twenty international flights.

How ironic, my parents thought glumly. The largest strike in Japan's history had stranded this union president's new baby. Perhaps Rollie's sympathies for the movement gave them the patience to get through this last hump. Chris and Rollie waited by the phone and watched the television, calling the airlines constantly.

The wait was torturous for Maureen, too. Most nuns never experience motherhood like she had. She had grown to believe she could understand my baby babble and that I, in a sense, could understand her. She was the only parent I knew. Maureen always believed that even though my birth mother had said that the adoption was the decision of both parents, Ma had not wanted to give me up. There was something in her eyes and her manner, the undeniable posture of yearning and loss. Maureen understood that feeling more and more.

Two days later, Japanese workers called off the strike when their government agreed to pay raises. Flights began to normalize. That night Maureen suffered a fit of anxiety and could not stop crying. In the morning, she and some other nuns took me to the airport, dressed in all the clothing that I owned. Maureen was beside herself as she handed me to the airline hostess who would fly with me overseas, but I was serene and smiley.

"It was almost as if she knew she was going," Maureen later wrote to my American parents. "As I watched the plane go off, all I could think of was 'my baby' was going to be in a normal family situation where she could have a mother's and father's love."

Maureen sobbed the entire bus ride back to Taitung.

TWO DAYS BEFORE Rollie's thirty-fifth birthday, on April 13, 1974, I arrived in the United States. I was almost eight months old. The doors of immigration opened and a woman appeared, holding a big fat bundle with a mop of wavy black hair. I was gurgling, smiling, swaddled in about fifteen layers of clothing, topped off with a red silk jacket. Chris snapped a picture of me with the Japan Airlines employee, who then disappeared into the bowels of the airport. Then we were three.

Chris had brought only one Kleenex in her purse. How much crying could she really do? But she wept uncontrollably and had to use her sleeve to dry her face. Rollie, unaccustomed to holding a baby, awkwardly took me into his arms, but I didn't cry. I just examined them curiously. They took me back to their hotel room and gave me a bath and dressed me in a flowery little dress that Rollie had chosen. I grunted and he ran to the side of my hotel crib to see what was the matter. Chris warned him not to spoil me. I crawled all over the bed and all over them. I whimpered, and they fed me. I pooped and they changed me.

Suddenly, we were a family: Dad, Mom, and child.

It happened so fast, after such a long wait. My mom said that only for one split second in that airport, I was a dark, foreign bundle, someone else's child. But once in their arms, I was theirs.

5

HAPPY DAYS

One of the first confessions that I can remember making to my parents was pronounced with fear and shame when I was almost three.

We lived in a white ranch home that we called the White House on Beech Daly Road in Taylor. We had a two-acre back-yard with lots of grass, an aboveground pool, a sandbox, and a swing set that my dad painted yellow. It was a sunny afternoon, and I was playing by myself in our living room while my mother cleaned in the kitchen. I could hear the sound of running water in the kitchen sink.

When I woke up that morning, I had asked mom to help me put on my favorite dress, a pale yellow floor-length number trimmed in front with bows and fringe. My mother had pulled my black hair into ponytails, accented with bows of thick, bright yellow yarn. I sat on the blue and black speckled loop carpet, playing my scenario over and over, talking it out with all the important parties. Mom heard my kid babble but couldn't make out what I was saying. Little did she know that I was planning and acting out an elaborate wedding ceremony with music and flowers and my own handsome groom.

Mom went on with her chores. Then I heard the motor of my

dad's car as he pulled into the driveway. I jumped up and wedged my body between the living-room window and the couch, a space I often turned to for hiding or toddler inner reflection. I hoped that my father would not find out what I had done during the day while he was gone.

I stood there, rustling the curtain and talking to myself.

Mom peeked behind the couch.

"Mei-Ling, what are you doing?" she asked.

"I can't tell you." I answered.

"Come on, honey, what's going on?"

I shook my head side to side.

"Mei-Ling . . ."

I was trapped. I had no choice but to give it up. I looked up with guilty eyes and responded in a loud whisper:

"I don't want Daddy to know I married Fonzie."

I SLIPPED INTO my American life easily, as if I was always meant to be there. I grew up on Gerber baby food and apples and bananas from Farmer Jack. My parents read me Dr. Seuss before bed and let me watch *Sesame Street*. I had an enviable collection of bathing suits and started swimming classes shortly after I arrived in the States. My room and my baby furniture were painted red, white, and blue, and my father hung large red wooden letters on the wall: MEI-LING. I was the center of my parents' world and had most of what I wanted even before I knew it. I was especially close to my father. It was, my mom said, love at first sight. Contrary to what Maureen predicted, my dad's plentiful facial hair never bothered me. I loved to sit on his chest, put my feet in his bushy beard, and laugh and laugh and laugh.

My mom and dad say I was a happy child, adaptable and good-humored most of the time, though stubborn and a little spoiled. I hated to sleep and once threw myself out of my crib—landing with a loud thud—seven times in one night. I learned to say my ABCs at two years of age. I ate and drank everything and was impossibly whiny and cranky when I was hungry. When we went to the beach and I felt thirsty, I would walk up to people's beach blankets and drink from their cups. I stayed with my baby-sitter, Zadia, during the day while my parents worked, but during the weekends my parents took me on bike rides or to Detroit Metroparks or to see my grandparents or to Greenfield Village in Dearborn, where I liked to feed popcorn to the carp. My parents and grandmothers made sure I was dressed to the nines, with a wardrobe that included plaid pants, frilly dresses, and a sweater-poncho with a bunny-eared hood.

We were a typical midwestern family with a very atypical look. In the 1970s Asian adoptions were still rare, although some families had begun adopting babies from Vietnam and South Korea. In Metro Detroit, where everyone was basically black or white, people gawked. Mom and Dad would wrap me up in my coat and hat and take me to the park or the grocery store, and people would stare, sometimes stopping to ask us questions. They often thought I was from Vietnam, because they had heard that war babies were coming to the United States. Once, a woman told my amused father that we looked alike, but Mom does not remember ever hearing an intentionally offensive remark. A local newspaper published a small story on us with the headline "China Doll." We were a novelty. Of course, back then I didn't know to know we were different. I probably loved the attention.

People often ask me when I found out I was adopted. For a long time, I was puzzled by that question because it was a no-brainer. How could I not know? My parents are Caucasian and I am Asian. It wasn't like they could hide our genetic differences. I cannot remember a time when I was "told" or in which I "heard." So I asked my mom if we ever had such a discussion.

"No," she told me. They always called me their "beautiful adopted baby."

"But *adoption* was just a word," she said. "We used it so you would know it, but it meant nothing to us. Everyone makes such a deal of it. I think it's crazy. Adopted is adopted. 'So what?' was always our feeling."

Never once in my life did I have a problem with that. I never felt separation pains that I can recall. I felt isolated racially at times, but the fact that I was not my parents' biological child was never an issue. Being adopted was just an obvious fact.

Besides, to my child mind, adoption seemed a plenty logical way for people to reproduce, way more reasonable than the idea that women grew babies in their bellies that popped out after forty weeks. It made all the sense in the world to me that we would pick up my new brother at the airport—I mean, that's where I came from, right?

MY PARENTS KNEW they wanted another child before they ever had me in their arms, but they didn't want to suffer through another touch-and-go private adoption experience. They turned to a local group called Americans for International Aid and Adoption, then a seedling organization run out of the Troy, Michigan, home of Nancy Fox, who had adopted a girl from Vietnam. The process was much less formal then; Nancy's contacts in other countries told her how many orphans they had, and she worked with the state of Michigan to place them.

I vaguely remember my parents explaining to me that my brother was coming from South Korea. I was three then, but my parents already talked to me as if I was a shrimp-sized adult. They made it clear I was to love him and help take care of him.

Ooooooh. A brother! (read: another toy). I'm sure my parents showed me that first picture they received of him, the one that still brings tears to our eyes. It is a small passport-sized photo in black and white. He is a sad child, with vacant eyes and fuzzy hair.

My parents decided early on that they would keep Hoon-Yung's Korean name, which orphanage officials had given him, just as they kept my given name. According to his papers, the name Hoon-Yung meant "brave, strong boy." My parents thought our Asian names were special, a small homage to our past, and used to get irritated when friends called me Mei for short. Too bad if Americans had to fumble around to pronounce them at times. *Is it Mary? Marilyn? Mee-Lang?*

I admit that I myself had a wee bit of trouble with my new brother's name at first. One day in gymnastics class, where I had been focusing on balance with an eye on more complicated moves such as somersaults, a friend of my mother's asked me, "What's the name of your new brother?"

I puffed out my chest with pride and declared, "Hong Kong Phooey!"

We met my new brother on July 10, 1976, in Detroit Metro Airport, only a few miles from our house. Mom dressed me up in a white sundress with white sandals for the occasion. We waited with my grandparents in the immigration hall of the airport for a couple hours before the doors swung open and a woman came out holding a skeleton of a child in her arms. Hoon-Yung was the last passenger off his flight. He could not hold up his head. He could not sit up. The agency had told my parents that he was about nineteen months old, but he was smaller than I had been when I arrived at half his age.

This can't be my son, my mom thought to herself. She was expecting a robust toddler, who was walking or at least ready to walk.

This can't be my son.

But it was. The plastic bracelet wrapped around his bony arm read CHUNG, HOON-YUNG. He was ghostly white, dressed in a light blue and white checkered jumper. His belly was enormously swollen. He did not smile, and we weren't sure if he knew how. Even if he had known, he would not have had the energy to do it. At the airport, he barely made a peep as my mom gathered his emaciated body close.

Hoon-Yung had been abandoned in the streets of Incheon, Korea, soon after he was born. He was placed in the Star of the Sea Orphanage, where he was well on the way to dying of starvation. Officials guessed his age because he had no medical records or even a note of who his family might be.

From my dad's arms, I watched anxiously. *What is wrong with this kid?* I was ready to grab, hug, kiss, and play—the last thing he wanted. After begging incessantly, I was allowed to hold him. My mother put that tiny child in my lap and I tried to prevent him from sliding out of my arms and down my legs. (As you can imagine, he was a little harder to manage than a doll, since he moved on his own and all.) Hoon-Yung showed little interest in me and instead played with two plastic airline cups.

We brought him home. For weeks, my brother acted as if he was still fighting for his life in Korea. When you spilled a handful of Cheerios in front of him, he would panic and madly grab at all the tiny circles, hoarding them close to his body. If he dropped anything on his bib, he would eat it immediately. Mom and Dad learned not to put out serving bowls with food because he would eat all the food in one panicked gulp. He hovered over food for months, until he finally realized there was enough. The memory of his terrified hunger still made Granny, my dad's mom, cry two decades later. My dad caught one of many illnesses that my brother suffered, and it took our father months to recover from a stomach infection that doctors never could identify.

Slowly but surely, Hoon-Yung got healthy and came out of his shell, thanks to the love and care of my parents, their friends, and our babysitter Zadia. They fed, hugged, and kissed him. They dressed him, read to him, and gave him toys. He smiled for the first time about five weeks after he arrived, when Zadia was playing on the floor with him. Then and there, the orphan began to disappear for good.

My mom credits to some extent his pushy sister for making him do stuff even if he didn't want to. I made him play with my Playskool *Sesame Street* people. I combed his hair. I sat him on the closed toilet, tied a towel around his neck, and brushed his teeth. I tried to teach him to boogie and sing. We played in the red baby pool outside, and I would try to teach him my version of going "underwater" (leaning back and dipping my hair in the water). It was just what he needed, Mom theorized, someone who was oblivious to his limits. I was just being bossy me.

We were inseparable back then, Hoon and me. We spent hours making cities of mud and sand and digging tunnels and swamps to drown our Matchbox cars in the sandbox. We swam practically every day almost every summer of my young childhood, cannonballing, playing Marco Polo, and turning golden brown under the Michigan sun. We nibbled watermelon at our picnic table and spit the seeds into the green grass. Hoon tolerated his big sister, although if I bugged him too much, he would throw me a nasty look—the same one he occasionally gives me to this day if I annoy him. Or he'd hit me in the head with a plastic boat, which today, fortunately, he does not do.

I WAS NINE years old when we adopted my second brother. We had moved from the White House three doors down to a home my dad had designed. It was much larger, with lots of large glass windows, a wood exterior, and a slanted roof. It sat back on a wooded two-acre plot of land. My parents' bedroom took up the entire second floor and included a walk-in closet, a terrace, giant picture windows, and a bathroom with a Jacuzzi and sauna that I liked to show my friends. My room was at the end of the house on the first floor. A bathroom separated my brothers' room from mine. The entire house was built to blend with its natural surroundings. We had squirrels, lots of birds, rabbits, and sometimes foxes. We also had the occasional Peeping Tom because back then our house was considered especially nice in a working-class town. People thought we were rich, but the home was merely the product of years of careful saving by my folks.

In fifth grade I was a perfect prepubescent mess. I had long black hair that I often tied into braids. I wore chunky glasses with purple-tinted plastic frames, and my favorite outfit, I regrettably recall, was a plaid maroon shirt with ruffles and burgundy culottes. I was especially young for my grade—I had skipped third grade and my birthday was in the summer, so I was at least a year or two younger than my classmates. I was beginning to notice how absolutely uncomfortable and awkward I was. The seed of self-loathing had begun to bud in my head. I wondered if a boy could ever like a Chinese girl. I never spoke about these worries to anyone, especially not to my parents, who had tried so hard to teach us to be proud of who we were and where we came from. I didn't think they would understand.

These doubts did not apply to my brother, however. So when my parents asked me if I wanted another sibling from Korea, I answered a resounding yes, though I vetoed the idea of a sister because I didn't want to share my bedroom.

Moon Jung-Hoe was the third addition to the Hopgood family. He was five when he walked off the airplane on September 9, 1982, grinning like mad as he held the hand of my dad, who had gone to Chicago to meet his international flight. He was thin and had a head of straw-stiff hair. A spray of brown freckles covered his flat nose, which spouted perfectly round beads of sweat when he got hot. Jung-Hoe was dressed in striped pants with red suspenders.

He was shockingly smiley, especially for a child who had been abandoned and found wandering the streets in Kwang Ju in the aftermath of a bloody civil uprising in the city in 1980. Jung-Hoe had been holding hands with an older child—we didn't know if it was a friend or sibling—and put in an orphanage. The adoption agency observed that he was a good-natured child, though reserved. But for the first several days there, he stared out the front window and cried, as if waiting for someone who would never come. He later lived in at least one foster home.

Now he was arriving in a strange place, where no one spoke his language and few people looked like him, but he was grinning from ear to ear. He smiled so hard and so big that his eyes seemed to disappear in his face.

"Can he see?" my grandma asked.

Hoon and I began right away to love and torture the child, telling him to say this and say that in English. On the way home from the airport, he fell asleep while repeating a barrage of words. "Car?" "Cah." "House?" "House." "Mei-Ling?" "Ma-Lang." The only English words he knew were *helicopter* and *Coca Cola*.

Jung-Hoe had a history and memories of his native land that I never had, but he couldn't express them to us. Or rather, he could, but we could not understand. He would sit cross-legged on the couch after his bath and just before bedtime, wearing his pajamas covered with little cars, and sing Korean songs. We would sit in front of him and listen, a rapt audience. He used to laugh like mad at my mother when she would try to pronounce Korean words from her English-Korean handbook, although he refused to speak Korean with any native speakers. He corrected our pronunciation of his name. We said Jung-HOE. He insisted his name was Moon (his last name) Jung-HA. (Later when he studied and became fluent in Korean, he proclaimed that he had been wrong—or we had misunderstood him—and we were to go back to calling him Jung-HOE.) He liked to wake very early and stand outside the bedroom of his poor adolescent sister and yell, "Ma-Lang! Wake up!" He was a pack rat, saving wrappers, magazines, and other junk, a habit he likely developed in the orphanage that continues today.

Once, in a park, Jung-Hoe was chasing seagulls. Mom and Dad let him go on with this normally futile child's game and continued to play Frisbee. Suddenly, a commotion of screaming squawks filled the air.

The child had managed to catch a bird, using popcorn as bait. It screamed and flapped its wings and tried to peck out my brother's eyes. A posse of gulls circled overhead, threatening a rescue attack. My mother hates birds, a phobia she acquired as a child when bats got into her house. She and my dad yelled, "Drop it! Drop it! Put it down!"

My brother didn't understand. He stood serenely holding out the screaming bird toward his new parents. Finally, after jumping up and down, motioning and insisting, they convinced him to release the bird, which flew away in a white huff. Jung-Hoe didn't see what all the fuss was about. He was just rounding up dinner.

Awake, Jung-Hoe expressed incredible joy and an astounding ability to learn and adapt. He ate everything he was given, and still does. He loved his preschool and promptly won the affections of the cutest blonde-haired, blue-eyed girl in his class.

But when he slept, his past emerged from its dark resting place and tortured him. At first he was unable to sleep on a bed—he was used to lying on the hard floor—so he often rolled or climbed down and curled up on the carpeted floor. He also would moan and scream in his sleep, and the chilling cries would resonate through the heat registers of our house. His night terrors regularly woke me out of a dead sleep. (On the other hand, Hoon learned to sleep through the outbursts, unmoved, in the bed next to him.) My parents or I would come into the room and embrace him. When we woke him, he sat up and smiled with tears in his eyes, never remembering what he had dreamed—or at least that's what he told us. It was like clockwork, at home or on family vacations. I have a clear image of my father's rising from his hotel bed in Florida and crouching on the floor next to a sobbing Jung-Hoe, caressing his head and murmuring reassurances. Jung-Hoe suffered from these fits for several months after his adoption, until one day the terrors just stopped. I always had the feeling that that evening in his dreams, he finally was able to close that tumultuous chapter in his life.

ON SUBURBAN DETROIT'S social ladder, Taylor occupied a rung somewhere near the bottom, and the people from neighboring suburbs loved to step on us, and hard. Teens from other towns quipped that we lived in "Taylortucky," referring to the large number of southerners who immigrated there, and claimed we lived in trailer parks, bought our clothes from Kmart, and parked our cars in our front yards. I did know a couple people who did those things, but mostly those were unkind and untrue stereotypes. Still, the Taylor I grew up in was a blue-collar city of auto assembly-line operators and foremen, office managers and teachers, of sports bars without windows, strip malls, and disconnected subdivisions. It was the perfect hometown for my dad, who fancied himself the champion of the worker and the underdog. He dedicated his life as a teacher and public official in the city to changing Taylor's reputation, pushing to improve public schools, bulldoze crime-ridden public-housing projects, and build parks and golf courses.

One thing was true: the city was mostly white. In the 1970s, when I arrived, Taylor's population was 90 percent white and about 9 percent black. Only about one percent was Asian; I figured my brothers and I made up a notable part of that one percent.

My parents did what they could to try to make up for that isolation. They tried to give us some kind of Asian experience by hanging Asian art on the walls and hiring Asian babysitters. They bought me an Asian Raggedy Ann doll, as well as a black Raggedy Andy doll, which were my favorite toys for years. We ate Chinese food regularly and drove to Ann Arbor to get Korean *bulgogi*. They sent my brothers to Korean school, which the boys despised except for the meals and the Tae Kwon Doe classes; they just didn't understand the lessons because neither spoke Korean. My parents offered to send me to Chinese school, but I refused. Back then, we just wanted to be seen as American.

On June 19, 1982, two drunk autoworkers named Robert Ebens and Michael Nitz beat Vincent Chin, a twenty-seven-year old Chinese American, to death. Chin had been in a Detroit strip club celebrating his last days as a bachelor when the three men got into an argument. Ebens and Nitz reportedly called Chin a "Jap," and Ebens said, "It's because of you, motherfuckers, that we're out of work!" All three got thrown out of the bar, and then Ebens and Nitz hunted Chin down and smashed his head with a baseball bat.

"It isn't fair," Chin gasped before he lost consciousness, according to court testimony. Four days later he died, five days before he should have married. Both men were acquitted because the prosecutor failed to show up. National mass protests inspired the Justice Department to retry the men and a jury found Ebens guilty of violating Chin's civil rights, but Ebens won on appeal and was set free.

The Chin case and the anti-Japanese sentiments that surged throughout the country and especially in Michigan in the early 1980s scared us. Automakers and workers blamed Japan's booming car industry for their woes, and politicians and pundits were glad to adopt a thinly veiled language of blame, anger, and hate. It was one thing to talk about unfair trade and competition—my father was prolific at that discourse—but it was much easier to target the yellow threat. The fact that they were talking about the Japanese made little difference to the uneducated and unexposed. To them, we "yellow, slant-eyed gooks" were all alike.

To be fair, my brothers and I never felt as if our physical safety was at risk. Most of the teasing we faced during our childhood was the silly, ignorant stuff of kids: the hiss of "ching-chang-chung," the kids who pulled back the ends of their eyelids, the chanting of "Chinese, Japanese, dirty knees, look at these!" Sometimes drunks in cars screamed, "Go back to your country!" Other times, it was what people didn't say: the nasty stares and suspicious looks. My parents tried to counter any racism. They did their best to explain ignorance and hate, dismissing the offenders as idiots. Had Dad witnessed any harassing, my anti-gun, Brady bill–loving father might have hunted down the offenders and shot them. But it's hard to avoid being stained by the ignorance of the people around you—ask any Asian American or other minority. On the mean streets of adolescence, you are on your own in the fight against your demons.

I wanted to be anything but Asian. I used to curse being different in my journals and in my dreams at night. I overcompensated. I went out of my way to prove how American I was, making sure people heard me speak my perfect English. I was Little Miss Everything in high school, class president for three years, captain of the pom-pom team, and a member of almost every club that existed. I excelled at a lot of things: school, socializing, public speaking, organizing. I had a healthy family life and lots of friends.

Yet I was a tormented hypocrite. Outwardly I tried to ignore or make light of the stereotypes and slurs. The one time our terrible advanced placement English class actually read a Shakespearean play, *A Midsummer Night's Dream*, I was accidentally cast as the "Chink in the Wall." I was horrified inside but giggled to deflect the anxiety I felt. I allowed myself to acquire the nickname "Chinky" —I think it began as a joke in pom-pom. I even painted it on my Buick Regal as part of my graduation graffiti. I would defend my brothers, but I would never have dated an Asian guy. During high school, I resisted even hanging around Asians. I did have one half-Korean friend who was on the pom-pom squad with me, but that was enough. To this day, I still feel bad for not being nicer or getting to know the only other Asian American in my high school classes, a terribly nice and smart guy, but I was so worried that I would be automatically paired with him in the minds of my friends that I kept my distance.

I watched the movie *A Christmas Story*, which I now find delightful, and felt hot and flushed during the part when thanks to the Bunkus's dogs, the family is forced to go to a Chinese restaurant for dinner. I cringed when the Chinese staff could not sing "Fa-la-la-la-la" and could only say "Fa-ra-ra-ra-ra."

That's me. That's what they think of me, I thought. They think because I look like this, I talk like *that*.

I worried when friends wanted to fix me up on dates.

"Do they know I'm Asian?" I asked anxiously, thinking that no one would possibly think I was attractive.

I got sick of people asking, "Where are you from?" and after hearing my answer, "Taylor, Michigan," their asking, "No, where are you *really* from?" I'd tell people I wanted to be a journalist and they almost always asked, "Like Connie Chung?" I grew bitter about Connie during my young years. I am not unlike many of my Asian American friends in this struggle, but I did not know that yet. Aside from Pat Morita on *Happy Days* and *The Karate Kid,* there weren't many Asian American stars, no Lucy Lius, no Amy Tans or Michelle Kwans. There were no rainbow casts like you'd see later on popular television series such as *ER, Lost,* or *Grey's Anatomy.* I felt isolated, and that would not change until my final years of college. I didn't discuss those feelings with my brothers or my parents until years later; I didn't want them to think they had done anything wrong. It was my problem, and mine alone.

6

THE RETURN

For two decades, Ma kept a picture of me on her bedroom table. I was wearing a blue shirt and a white diaper. Sprouts of dark hair stuck out from my red knit cap. I had just arrived in the United States and was sitting on the hotel bed in San Francisco.

"Who's that?" my siblings asked occasionally, pointing at the picture.

"That is your sister," Ma and Ba answered humbly. They said little more for they knew almost nothing.

Years passed and many things had changed for my Chinese family. After giving me up, my parents had two more girls, one they kept and another they gave to a couple in Switzerland. Ba got into real estate and began earning more money. Little by little, they were able to claw their way out of poverty and into the middle class. The other daughters grew up, graduated from high school. Ba pushed them to study and helped to pay for their college. Meanwhile, the letters from Sister Maureen, who left Taiwan for Africa not long after I was adopted, tapered off.

My birth parents said that from time to time they inquired at St. Mary's Hospital, to see if any word had come from me or our Swiss sister; they didn't know how to contact me. Once, after Ma was severly injured in a moped accident, she asked for me while lying in her hospital bed, delirious. Another time, when our grandmother was on her deathbed the year before we made contact, Ba asked the nurses and priests to see if they knew anything more about my whereabouts.

"No, *dui buqi*," they said. We're sorry.

(I wonder now how they could not find me. We had moved only once during my childhood, only three houses away.)

Then, one early January day in 1997, a priest from St. Mary's called the Wang house.

"We have a letter," he told Ba. "You should come by."

Ba hurried into downtown Taitung. A nurse told him that Sister Maureen had made an inquiry to the hospital on my behalf. Ba asked the nurse to write a letter in English—he knew none—and rattled off updates on each family member, some of which were vaguely wrong in his haste or incorrectly translated. He gave ages, where they lived, where they worked. He insisted that I try to return for Chinese New Year, just one month away, and included a self-addressed envelope so I could easily respond.

"Tell her she has a whole family in Taiwan waiting anxious to meet her."

Their reasons for giving me up always seemed to be worthy. Surely, I must have a happy life and better opportunities. Surely, they made the right decision.

But to finally know. To get the chance to say the things that were never said.

"Tell her I will pay," Ba told the nun. "Tell her I will pay for her trip to Taiwan."

He rushed home to spread the news and called each of my sisters.

"We found her."

Soon, they hoped, their American daughter would come home.

IT WAS SURREAL, having my birth family in my life again. ("Again," I say, as if I actually acknowledge that they had been in my life before.) Until those first letters, those first phone calls, I barely recognized that I could have had a life outside my family in the United States. Suddenly, I had seven sisters, six of whom were writing me an e-mail or a letter almost daily during that February and March of 1997. They all had studied some English, fortunately, because I knew no Chinese. We traded stories of our lives and our jobs, our boyfriends and families. We discussed our tastes in men, food, and music and even compared height and weight, blood type, and bra size.

Jin-Zhi, who was twenty-five—two years older than me— wrote most often because she seemed to know the most English. She was working in public relations for a recycling company and lived with my parents in Taitung. She told me that she had wanted to be a journalist, but Ba had forbidden her to work as a reporter, for her safety. She was hoping to pass the difficult exam to become a teacher.

She and the others peppered me with questions: Did I like Chinese food? Could I describe my "environment"? Did Americans wear Chinese clothing? Could I use chopsticks? Did I have my ears pierced? I asked lots, too: What did my sisters do at work? Where did they live? How was our family doing financially? Was our family close to one another?

I asked about our medical history; during doctor appointments I always completed forms asking for my family history with one word: *unknown*. Now, I finally could find out. Jin-Zhi told me our mother had suffered from cervical cancer, probably from having too many babies. She was recovering. A grandmother had died of lung cancer because she smoked too much, and an uncle had died of liver cancer because he drank too much.

Then, feeling emboldened, I asked a question that had nagged me since I was a teenager: did my mother or any of my sisters have a big chest?

I knew it might seem ridiculous or superficial, but the origin of my body type had been one of vexing questions of my youth. My first training bra, of the Strawberry Shortcake variety, started to fill out when I was eleven years old. By the time I was in high school, I was five feet two inches with a full C cup. My breasts were by no means huge, especially compared with my busty friends, but they were much larger than I had ever seen on any Asian person. My legs also seemed thicker than those of many Asians; Asian actresses always seemed so petite and willowy to me, as if the wind might topple them over. I was by no means fat, but I was sturdy. I always wanted to know if this was a genetic trait or if my figure came from the pizza and french fries I loved to eat. Any of my other friends could just look at their mom, dad, or sisters and say, "Yeah, well I know where *that* comes from." Not me. It was as if I had been beamed in from outer space. I could not have been more physically different from my mom, who was thin and white, with blonde hair and blue eyes.

So I asked the question, and as I had hoped, my sisters took it in stride—in fact they all got a big kick out of it. Jin-Zhi told me that some of our sisters were chesty and that we got it from our mother. My fourth-oldest sister, Jin-Hong, wrote: "HAHA! That's so funny. Sisters always talked about my chest but they will talk about you. Right? It's a joke. Don't be mind. It's an honor to us."

My sisters also passed along requests from my parents. For example, Ba wanted me to bring him "fish oil" for his digestive problems if I came back to Taiwan. One of the most fervent and amusing entreaties that Jin-Zhi relayed to me, almost immediately after contacting me, was that I was to buy clothing for our brother, the one that my birth parents had adopted shortly before giving me up.

"He is very fat," Jin-Zhi wrote. She explained that finding clothing for him in Taiwan was very difficult and Ba wanted me to bring him something to wear.

My family's requests and comments were blunt, forward, and confusing, but they amused me. I did not bump heads yet with the strong, stubborn personalities that characterize my family, nor did my sisters talk of the sordid family backstory that had haunted them. We were basking in the glory of discovery. I never had sisters. Their urgency became contagious. I felt as if I was being passionately recruited for an exclusive, mysterious sorority, and I was eager to be inducted officially into the club.

I decided to go back at the end of March 1997.

WHAT DO YOU PACK in your bag when you are going to meet your birth family in the country you left as a baby, in the home that was never really your home? What outfits and shoes do you wear? What gifts do you take? Which words do you learn in Mandarin to help you navigate the years and worlds that have grown up between you? I had taken some last-minute language classes. I could say basic things such as "hello," "good-bye," "thank you," "I love you," "I'm full," and "one pineapple cake, please." It was the best I could do for now.

Two days before I left for Taiwan, I unfolded, folded, and piled clothes on my bed. I was packing some of my favorites: a red and white picnic-table patterned shirt with short ruffled sleeves, sarongs, a brown button-down polyester shirt, a long khaki skirt, jean shorts: nothing special, but all flattering. The weather would be warm and humid during the day, my sisters said, and a little cold at night. I figured that a little cold to sisters who had spent their entire lives on a tropical island meant something quite different than it would to a girl from Michigan.

Almost half the space in my luggage was filled with presents. Chinese American friends had advised me that it was good form to bring presents for not only your family but for anyone you might meet, even something small, like candy or a pen. It had been a nightmare trying to find cheap trinkets that were genuinely made in America. I went to Target, Hudson's, and other stores. I dejectedly checked every tag looking for something that might be representative of the United States. It seemed like every stuffed animal, every toy, every piece of clothing was made in Taiwan, China, or another Asian country. I did manage to find a cute jumper with a red, white, and blue flag for my fourth sister's new baby girl. In the end, most of my gifts were nothing special. For my birth mother, I chose citrus soaps and lotions from the Body Shop, and for my sisters, smaller packets of bath gels and beads, body puffs, and back washers. (To my chagrin, I would see a Body Shop along a busy street in Taiwan.) I had found my brother large clothes—sweatpants and khakis and three shirts. I bought *St. Louis Post-Dispatch* T-shirts at my newspaper's souvenir shop for my brothers-in-law and a black *Post-Dispatch* tie for my birth father—cheesy, but local. For random relatives, I bought Hershey's kisses, wrapped them in cellophane and tied the packets with red and white ribbons.

My American parents gave me a coffee-table book on Michigan to present to my Chinese parents. We had shopped together when I had returned home to Detroit a few weeks before leaving for Taiwan.

Throughout these weeks, Mom and Dad always seemed more excited than I was about the reunion. I tried to include them in the experience as often as I could by calling them when I heard from my birth parents and reading them letters from my sisters.

Mom told me she flinched just once when she considered my birth parents.

"Mom," I said showing her a picture, "This is my mother."

How could there be another mother? she thought.

But after that, she took it in stride.

"How do you feel about this?" I asked her.

"I'm very excited for you," she deadpanned. "But when you get back you have to make sure to tell me how much younger I look and how much prettier I am than your mother."

My grandmother told me before I left, "Remember, I will always be your granny."

Still, I was careful not to say anything I thought might hurt my parents. For a long time, I tried to avoid calling my Chinese parents "my" parents. I referred to them as "the" parents, "the" father, and "the" mother. Sometimes I slipped.

At first, my dad thought that he and my mom should go with me to Taiwan, but I knew right away that I wouldn't be comfortable with that. I'd be too worried about what the Hopgoods were thinking and feeling to concentrate on getting to know the Wangs. I remember rehearsing the conversation with my dad in my head before calling him from St. Louis. *Dad, I think I should travel to Taiwan on my own. I know you know you will always be my true parents, but . . .*

Yet as soon as I mentioned that it might be best if I went alone, Dad said, "That's fine."

"We understand," he told me. "But someone should still go with you. How about Sister Maureen? We could pay for her ticket."

I asked Maureen and she graciously accepted. It was settled: my birth parents would pay for my flight, and my adopted parents would pay for hers.

As a final gift to my birth family, I decided to put together a photo album. Photos seemed the best way to show them a bit of what my childhood, my adolescence, and my family were like. Mom and Dad wholeheartedly agreed, and on my visit home we spread their photo albums and hundreds of old pictures on the brown living-room carpet and began sorting. I always loved to leaf through those old books with the psychedelic, 1970s-style green, blue, purple, and white covers and the crinkling plastic photo slips. We picked though the precious memories in our history, lingering, laughing, and reminiscing.

We chose photos of me after I arrived in San Francisco and became part of the Hopgood family: me, hugging my Asian Raggedy Ann doll; Mom holding me after she put my ponytails in curlers; my new Korean brother, Hoon-Yung, and me, standing knee deep in Michigan snow, so bundled up in winter coats that our arms looked stiff; me posing in my green tutu, hamming it up as usual; Dad helping me do my homework; the arrival of Jung-Hoe, at five years old, at the airport, grinning as he clutched his favorite stuffed bear, Cherry; me with big, frighteningly flammable 1980s hair in high school prom pictures. There were first Halloweens, first Santa Claus visits, first days of school, and college graduations. We giggled over the bell-bottomed hipster style of my parents, the bowl haircuts of our youth, my forced toothbrushings of my brother, and my unflinching knack as a child for showing off my (often ruffled) underwear.

"Am I taking too many pictures?" I asked my mother. Didn't they want to keep some of these photos for themselves?

"Take what you want, honey," Mom said. "We've got lots."

ON THE MORNING of Friday, March 28, 1997, my boyfriend drove me to the St. Louis airport. I would fly through Detroit, meet Sister Maureen, and we would continue to Taiwan with a short stop in Japan. I made a point of trying to record everything I could in my diary and notebooks.

8:03 a.m. *I am sitting in Gate 3 of Lambert Airport waiting to board the flight. Monte, tired mussy-haired boy that he is, dropped me off. I adore him. He is so disheveled—flannel this way, hair that way, smelling like the Bass Ale he drank at King Louie's last night—but as sweet as can be. He bought me a neck cushion and a soft handle to pull my luggage. I adore him. Maybe I love him.*

Right now I feel . . . tranquil. Like I better not get excited because it's a long, long trip. I think I still feel a little disbelief, kinda outside my body instead of being in the guts of what's happening today/tomorrow. In exactly 24 hours I am to walk off this plane and meet the parents I left almost 23 years ago.

9:30 p.m. CST. *Flying over the vast Pacific Ocean. A smaller plane is leaving a puffy line of smoke to the south of us. We are headed West to get East. How true.*

So far I think Sister Maureen and I are going to be fine. She is kind and very friendly and open-minded. She is trying to sleep finally now. I think I may be done sleeping. My eyes are tired but I can't seem to drift off. I do wonder what [my family will] think of me, and I hope it is good. I think the healthiest way to look at all this is to think that they are friends. New and great friends. Will we hug? Laugh? Cry? Will my emotional "wall" lift? I feel as if I should be feeling more.

2:15 a.m. CST, 5:12 p.m. Japan time in Narita Tokyo National Airport. *I just washed my face and wet my hair and brushed my teeth so I feel like half a new woman, anyway. Everyone around us is Asian. How cool.*

4:30 a.m. CST. *My journal just fell apart and I'm pretty sure I've reached the state of pure, absolute exhaustion. On my flight to Taipei. I'm sitting in Row 22, Seat G, reciting, "Wo shi nida* nuer. Wo hen gaosheen hui dao jia" *(I am your daughter. I am very happy to have come home). I am pooped to the point where I think it is extra hard to concentrate.*

4:45 a.m. CST. *I spoke my first Chinese to someone I do not know. The stewardess asked me in Chinese if I wanted café—or* cha *(tea) or orange juice and then gave the English translation. And I said,* "Cha. Xiexie" *(Tea. Thank you). She answered,* "Bu kequi" *(You're welcome). Yeah! The simplest things make me happy.*

6:30 a.m. CST. OK. *So we're half an hour away from Taipei and I just took a long nap but I have a fishy taste in my mouth from the salmon dinner. And I'm dressed now but my hair looks like complete shit. I don't know why I did not have the foresight to curl my bangs. So basically my hair is going to look horrid at this sacred moment. Terrific . . .*

Well, here's goes nothing.

We landed, hurriedly grabbed our things and made for the exit.

Okay, now I am nervous.

We stopped in the airport bathroom and splashed cold water on our faces. I stared at myself in the mirror. Indeed, my hair was deformed, eyes baggy. I was hot, sweating even.

Oh God. I look awful.

"How do you feel?" asked Maureen.

"Fine," I snapped at her. She understood; she was nervous for me. I was shaking inside as I handed Maureen my camera.

"I hope I can get more than just your back," she mumbled. We hurried down the sparkling pink and white tiled corridor and toward the baggage claim.

• • •

ALMOST THE ENTIRE FAMILY had gathered in Chiang Kai-shek International Airport: parents, sisters, brothers-in-law, and children. They had written MEI-LING on a sign and bought a fake plastic flower lei to throw over my shoulders when I arrived.

They fidgeted. Ba paced back and forth. My fourth sister, Jin-Zhi, filmed everyone and everything. She would record this scene on tape and later give a copy to me.

"Look, Ma," she said, pointing the camera her way. "Look how pretty you look."

"Stop it!" Ma snapped. She had chosen a yellow and green flowered top and a scarf, and wore bright red lipstick.

"I will not cry, I will not cry," she repeated to her daughters.

MAUREEN AND I STOOD among the chaos just beyond the customs exit, scanning the crowd for a familiar face. We looked to the left, and two men were waving furiously. I recognized them from pictures. My brother-in-law. My father.

"Mei-Ling-Ah!"

My sisters practically shoved my Chinese parents my way.

"Ni hao," I said as Ma walked up to me and burst into tears. We hugged, and then Ba embraced me, crying. I let out a sob and was surprised by my own sorrow.

We squeezed each other's hands for an awkward instant, celebrating and mourning everything that had happened and was happening. Ma turned away, trying to compose herself.

I had no time to think or catch my breath. Sisters, nieces, and nephews were hurdling my way. I suddenly had the lei around my neck and an unruly mob consumed me.

I am Jin-Hong. I am Jin-Zhi. I am Jin-Feng. Jin-Xia. Jin-Qiong. I am Min-Wei. This is my son. This is my daughter. This is my husband. Take a picture with your nephew, Hong-Yu. Can you say Mei-Ling Aiyi (Auntie Mei-Ling)? How was your flight?

Are you hungry? Why you have such big eyes? We go now to Jin-Feng house. You hungry? Do you want something to eat?

I tried to speak in Mandarin to my mother, to say, "I am very happy to come home," but she looked at me blankly. One of my sisters translated, repeating what I had said correctly, with the right inflection. Ma smiled. She worried that I was chilly, although I was wearing long sleeves and a long skirt. She pointed to me, wrapped her arms around herself and feigned a shiver. She told my sisters she felt cold just looking at me.

MAUREEN AND I CRAMMED into a black car with Ba, Ma, and a brother-in-law for the trip to the home of my oldest sister, Jin-Feng, in Hsinchu. Because she was still acclimating to Chinese, Sister Maureen couldn't translate the long strings of conversation that passed between everyone in the car. I began to sulk, staring out the window, cursing myself for not learning more Mandarin.

Suddenly, Ba turned to me and started talking so fast it seemed as if he'd burst. Maureen translated the best she could.

"He says that he liked what he had heard when I told him about your mother and father," she said.

"We had too many children," Ba explained. "We had a hard life and were very poor. We wanted to give you a better life, so we gave you up, but it still broke our hearts."

Pause.

"I want you to know. I hope you understand."

I expected this moment. I had practiced my response with a tutor and on the plane. I wanted to be sure I was understood. For now, I was open. For now, I meant what I said. The doubts would not come until later.

"*Meiguanxi. Wo ai nimen.*" It doesn't matter. I love all of you.

Ba's eyes welled with tears.

BIG AND BRIGHT SIGNS in Chinese characters lit up the night. Cars and mopeds carelessly swerved in and out of traffic. We were sharing the road with millions of crazy people, I thought, as I stared wide-eyed at this exotic world.

We arrived at the house of my oldest sister, jumped out of the car and waited outside holding our bags. Ba barked orders, arguing with Ma and the sisters. Jin-Xia told me not to mind his nervous fidgeting.

"He just want to make this night perfect," she said.

We walked through a ceramic tiled courtyard to the apartment. Before we entered, we took off our shoes and put on plastic house slippers. My sisters sat me down in the middle of a black leather sofa. They insisted that my mother sit next to me and they squeezed in nearby. Suddenly I was part of that pile of sisters, and of nieces and nephews, who were hoisted onto my lap, forced to pronounce my name and give me hugs.

"Say 'I love you, Auntie,'" they were told.

"I luh-vah you, Ahn-tee," they squeaked.

Jin-Feng, pregnant with her second daughter, brought out a porcelain tea set. Her husband poured the steaming water from the regular pot to a fancy clay pot and then into tiny cups.

"To family," they said, raising their cups. "To being together again."

They fed me pastries filled with chunks of meat, and giant, dripping pork dumplings. They were both impressed and amused with the way I used my chopsticks. (I usually hold one chopstick like you might hold a pencil, braced between the tip of my middle finger and the knuckle of my thumb; the other I maneuver up and down with the top of my thumb and my index finger.) They made me talk on the phone to an uncle and my older brother, who waited for my arrival in Taitung, even if I couldn't speak Mandarin. They took pictures and filmed every move I made.

They showered me with gifts. Jin-Feng gave me a jade necklace and ladybug earrings. Jin-Xia got me a teapot set engraved with dragons. Jin-Zhi gave me CDs of Chinese pop music. The booty piled on the table in front of me: secondhand jewelry, a huge sack of peanut candy from Kinmen Island, Chinese-language books, tapes, and even an electronic Chinese-English translator (I got the hint). Ba gave me a red envelope with one thousand U.S. dollars to cover most of my plane trip.

Offerings of welcome, offerings of guilt, I thought. I wanted to pass out my gifts, but my sisters would not let me.

"This is your time," they said. "Tomorrow you can give."

"Ba want to buy you your gold jewelry for when you marry," they said. I told them this was not necessary because I did not plan to wed anytime soon. They ignored me.

They proclaimed that I looked like the fourth sister, Jin-Hong, and Min-Wei, who sat nearby, grinning. Min-Wei was a year younger than me. She had long hair, highlighted red, and olive skin. Like me, she looked more like our father, with the same nose, chin, and brow.

"Min-Wei always say she is number one best-looking sister, but now you number one," one sister said.

Min-Wei laughed. "You like KTV?" She asked.

"KTV?"

"Karaoke."

"Ummmm." I paused, and then said, "Sure."

She loved karaoke, something I could not imagine doing unless good and buzzed. Min-Wei told me she liked to sing Toni Braxton's "Unbreak My Heart," and that she and her Australian boyfriend, Patrick, sang Paul Simon's "50 Ways to Leave Your Lover" in a karaoke contest, which they ended up winning.

Next came the presentation of the cake, a pillow-sized monster covered with fresh fruits, including bright green melon pieces, orange peaches, and ruby red strawberries on pale purple icing. The cake was in honor of my arrival and my oldest brother-in-law's fifty-sixth birthday.

Ba sat on the corner of the couch, observing and hovering. He wanted badly to speak with me, to ask me questions, to tell me what to do as he did to everyone else. Little did I know what a blessing it was to not understand. Ba made one of the sisters translate.

"Ba want to know how much money you make."

I raised my eyebrows, but my friends back in the United States and my Asian American literature had prepared me for these types of questions, so I answered: about thirty-eight thousand dollars. Ba calculated this in his head and laughed and announced that I made more than my brother-in-law, who is an engineer.

Then he asked me how much I paid for my apartment. About five hundred dollars a month, I told him.

"You pay too much," he said.

By the time all the food and the questions and conversation ended, it was about three in the morning. Maureen and I were beat, achy, and tired from the long journey. We were given the pink bedroom of Jin-Feng's daughter. The rest of the family would cram into the other bedroom and living room, sleeping together on beds and the floor, like they had as children. I listened to low talking and the clap of slippers on tile as I lay on my niece's rock-hard bed. A giant poster of Woody from *A Toy Story* stared down from the wall and a McDonald's Happy Meal box sat on her desk.

Before I drifted off, I heard Maureen's voice, distant and soft in the darkness: "I don't think I've ever seen a Chinese man cry."

I WOKE TO THE SOUND of roosters. The exhaustion of the day before had not worn off, but excitement did not allow me

to sleep any longer. We were going on a picnic. We had to take pictures first. I posed with everyone, in every possible combination—
with my parents, with just Ba, with just Ma, with my sisters, with
my brothers-in-law, with each sister and her family, with each
niece and nephew. Then at the park we did the same. I am sure
there is not one undocumented moment from that visit.

Then we began a unbelievable feeding frenzy that would not
end until I stepped back onto the plane.

I have always loved—obsessed over—food. I plan my life
around food. I apparently have always been this way. When I was
little, I would pester my parents with loud, insistent proclama-
tions of hunger at inappropriate times and always remembered
places according to the food I consumed. I may not remember
the name of the people we met or the monuments we visited on
a family outing, but I remember what we ate. The buttery corn
at former Congressman Bill Ford's annual fund-raiser. The hot
dogs at Tiger Stadium. The oranges on a trip to California. When
I go to different cities, I plan in advance what I will eat. Home to
Detroit? A Coney Island and chili fries, or *avegolemeno* soup and
flaming cheese in Greektown, or crushed lentil soup and *fattosh*
salad at any Lebanese restaurant. New York? Soup dumplings.

I love to cut grocery coupons from the Sunday newspaper, not
because I will buy these food products, but because I can *think*
about eating them. I always buy several restaurant guides for
whatever city I live in and relish each as if it is a favorite novel.
My husband dreads when it's my turn to order at restaurants
because I almost always have trouble deciding. I grill waiters on
the daily specials, just so I can imagine them. Choosing means
having to eliminate other potentially delicious options.

In Taiwan I fit right in. Eating is an event, a vital part of the
culture. People greet each other, not by asking, "How are you?"
but "Have you eaten?" When my family was not eating a meal,

they were snacking. When they were not snacking they were talking about the next meal. We ate beef noodles, whole white fish, spare ribs, shallot pancakes, rice porridge, eel, frog, dim sum, and tofu. We had shrimp dumplings, pork dumplings, boiled dumplings, and pan-fried dumplings. We had sushi, sashimi, fish ball soup, and spring rolls that you wrap in lettuce and eat with your hands. We drank soy milk, bubble tea, orange juice, guava juice, and the occasional Taiwan Beer. We snacked on Chinese star fruits, kiwis, apples, and sweet bean cakes. We ate in kitchens, in dining and living rooms, at Japanese and Hong Kong restaurants, in cars, on benches, and during walks.

I ate most everything they put in front of me. It took me a while to learn to leave a bit of food in my bowl to show that I could eat no more. Only a couple times did I taste something I could not stand. A family member bought me a fish cake, a crowd favorite in Taiwan. I took one bite and almost vomited. When the woman was not looking I spit my mouthful into a bush and threw away the remains. I declined trying the chicken feet that my oldest sister slurped and snacked on. I also passed on stinky tofu; a delicacy to many, it reeked to high heaven to me.

If I remarked that something was tasty, I got more of it than I could possibly eat. I mentioned I liked *fenglishu,* the pineapple cakes that I had tried at my Chinese tutor's house in St. Louis, mostly because it was one of the few words I could say. I ended up receiving several ornate boxes to take home.

Really, if I admired anything aloud, Ma, Ba, or my sisters tried to give it to me.

"What pretty teapots you have."

Ba opened the cabinet and offered one as a gift.

"No! No! No!"

They even tried to give things I didn't admire. At one point, Ba tried to give me a dozen toothbrushes.

"*Buyao! Xiexie! Buyao!* I don't want. Thank you," I weakly protested.

My sisters came to the rescue, chastising him. He finally retreated, disappointed.

"Tell Ba you want the car," Jin-Xia said, laughing.

"He isn't upset, is he?" I asked.

"Don't worry," she said. "He just want to give you everything."

EVERYWHERE I LOOKED, everywhere I went, everything I did, there were sisters. They hovered, doted, teased, bossed, laughed, and cried. They were my translators and tour guides, my keepers, protectors, and friends.

In the United States I had two younger brothers, but in Taiwan I was a *meimei*, a little sister, and I behaved like a *meimei*. At times, I would tickle my sisters or pull on their hair. We would walk down the street, and they would hold my hand, as many Chinese women do. During meals, they sat on both sides of me putting things that I did and did not want into my tiny bowl. Jin-Xia tried to correct the way I held chopsticks and my rice bowl. She cupped the bowl in one hand, delicately, with the pinkie pointing outward. "Beautiful," she said. She also scolded me for blowing my nose too loudly or spitting in the street (when I had caught a cold and could not help it). They all taught me words, phrases, games, and songs. One of our favorites was "*Ni shi wode jiemei, Ni shi wode beibei.*" You are my sister. You are my baby.

They took me to sing karaoke. We crammed into the small, private room and ordered rounds and rounds of food. I watched, amazed, as they sang one song after another in Chinese and in English. They played "Unbreak My Heart" and made Patrick, Min-Wei's then boyfriend, now husband, and me sing together. We sang "One Fine Day" and "Careless Whispers." I sang "Like a Virgin," glancing warily at Sister Maureen, and noticed with relief and amusement that she was singing, too. On my second night in Taipei, four sisters took me to the famous Shihlin Night Market. We took the light rail train to downtown after drinking a couple cans of Taiwan Beer. On the way, I taught Jin-Hong, whose face was flushed with alcohol, the word *buzzed*. I remember she was wearing a flattering summer dress, heels, and her husband's oversized warm-up jacket, and she tended to prolong the "zzzz" part of the word and raise her voice, pronouncing the word like a coy question.

"Buzzzzzed?"

After huddling together on the busy train, we burst through the Shihlin station turnstiles to join the fray that is the night market. Thousands of people milled in and out of the brightly lit open storefronts, where loud speakers blared rap music, and empty, recorded voices promised the best quality and the best discounts. Bright blue, orange, red, yellow, and white signs with neat, sweeping Chinese characters lit up the sky. Street vendors sold drinks with what looked like hunks of jelly floating on their surfaces, fruit piled on ice, and cherry tomatoes and boiled quail eggs alternately perched on sticks. Cooks poured dough and other more gooey and mysterious products into oily woks. The steam shot past the makeshift lights swinging above their stands and into the air in a greasy poof!

The black-market vendors, the ones who did not have licenses or shops, sold their contraband from rolling racks and ratty blankets that could be swept up and whisked away at the first sniff of police. The crowd swarmed around what I like to call hoochie clothing: tight tops, low-rise jeans, and the teeniest miniskirts. Giddy girls eagerly bought English T-shirts that often did not make sense; the shirts always seemed to feature spelling and phrasing that ranged from slightly off to flat-out nonsensical like "Destiny Girl Love Diamond" and "Bubble Star."

As foreign as all of this seemed—the food, the smells, the places, the faces, the language—I felt at home. We linked arms and swung into the crowd, almost skipping, and paused only to glance at a cute pair of high-heeled shoes, to shake our hips to the bass of a hip-hop song. We squeezed through the bustle like a snake, each of us holding tight to the next sister's hand. I could hardly breathe.

We were intrigued with each other's body parts. My sisters were perplexed by my "big eyes." I always thought I had average-looking, slanted Asian eyes. But they thought mine were abnormally large and round.

"Did you cut?" they asked, referring to the operations that some Asians get to make their eyes look larger. A doctor basically slices the eyelid to give it a crease, thus making the eye look rounder and more European. Ba piped in that I had the prettiest eyes of any of the sisters because they were so big. My sisters protested to his prejudiced standard of beauty and then theorized that my more American look must come from the food in the States.

I was overjoyed to see that a couple sisters had breasts like mine, that I was not some freak of nature.

"It is from mother," they teased, each claiming the other was bigger, poking and grabbing. We discussed and analyzed our faces, hands, calves, and butt sizes. We even compared feet. Each of us has a split toenail on our smallest toe. I always thought mine was ugly and strange. I hated to show my feet in sandals. Min-Wei showed me hers proudly.

"We all have. Little one!" she exclaimed, grinning, pointing.

I would never be ashamed again.

7

A PERFECT REUNION

We wanted to be perfect for each other. And for the moment, we were.

We knew each other enough to like each other and too little to annoy each other. We were funny and loud. We were happy faces, hugging father, mother, sisters and daughters, curious interviewers and interviewees. They asked invasive questions and I answered with a smile. I pried and they responded as best they could. We reached out and touched each other without hesitation. We wanted to accept and be accepted.

We were the lost and found, and the joy of recovery and discovery trumped regret, loss, or any other sad or shameful secrets that just weren't worth bringing up yet. They seemed to believe I was too good to be true, and they were right. Because of my poor Chinese, my politeness, and my desire to keep an open mind and make a good impression, my birth parents thought I was obedient and soft-spoken (an idea that made my American parents guffaw). They thought I was beautiful, but I believed I was no more appealing than any of my other sisters. My mother even told Maureen that I must be good because I accepted her, and she didn't think her other daughters would have tried to find her.

I refrained from telling her that for much of my life I had barely thought about her.

Perfection, of course, is never a permanent state. Humans are too complicated, our faults and failures bubbling in our blood, haunting us during our best as well as our worst times. This family had a dark side that crippled the hearts of its women, brought them to furious tears, and made them bull-headed and strong. But this reunion was not the time to air grievances. This was a time for celebration.

For now, we were just ecstatic to be together.

For now, we were a perfectly reunited family.

TAIPEI SPRANG UP in a basin that used to be a lake, and today it is an ultramodern sprawl of high-rises. Random English phrases hover among the Chinese characters above the packed sidewalks. Delicious Restaurant. KTV. Barbershop. Streets buzz with the latest cool cars and bikes to come out of Japan. Two and a half million people, most of them Han Chinese, live on top of each other in gray apartment buildings. What was simply everyday life to my family felt new and exhilarating to me. I loved when Min-Wei would put me on the back of her moped and we would fly down the streets, the smell of exhaust blasting our noses, our hair mussing and mingling in the hot wind. I liked being small and anonymous, the same as everyone else. Most people were short, and I was of average height. Everyone had dark hair and dark eyes, so they *tried* to make themselves different. They dyed their hair blonde, red, or orange, and they wore loud colors and mismatched patterns. The Chinese did not seem demure, as the stereotypes might imply. They were boisterous, whether bargaining over prices, ordering food, joking with friends, or arguing over a car accident. It all sounded the same to me.

Getting around Taiwan with my birth family was an elaborate

production. Maureen and I would get into the car. One or two sisters would put their children in with us. We would sit for a second, waiting for who knows what. Then, for no particular reason, those sisters would get out, rearrange, and a different niece would be thrust into our laps and a different sister would squeeze into the car. This would happen a few times before we started moving. And an hour later the caravan stopped and the changes started again. At first the disorder made me nervous. Driving with my American family to places such as Florida had been incredibly straightforward: little brother on the hump in the middle and ranking sister and brother on both sides. Play car games, sing a song, push each other around a little, get scolded, stop briefly and start again.

After a few days of touring the temples, parks, and landmarks of Taiwan, we traveled to Taitung. Maureen and I flew with Ma and Ba and a couple sisters, while the other members of the family drove. I almost did not make it onto the plane because Ba, instead of putting my actual, legal name on my airplane ticket, wrote Wang Mei-Ling, as if I still belonged to them.

MA AND BA'S HOUSE in Taitung was much larger than I imagined. A corrugated metal façade hid the three-story home. We entered a small alcove where we left our outdoor shoes, then passed through the front door into a large living room. On the walls hung a black clock, a hodgepodge of Chinese calendars, scrolls, and pictures of the family. Beyond the living room was a small dining room with a circular table in the center and beyond that a cluttered kitchen. The tub in the first-floor bathroom had no curtains or doors; a plastic hose and shower head was connected to a faucet that spat out a trickle of warm water for bathing.

Upstairs on the second floor were a few bedrooms and another small bathroom. As I wandered the hallways, I tried to imagine what it must have been like to grow up there, to know by heart the sound of our mother's shuffle down the hallway, the slam of the screen door as one of my siblings came home from school, a hard rain on the metal rooftop. I tried to conjure up some kind of intimacy with this place as I breathed in the smells of overripe vegetables and fruits, of fish and grease, of sweaty children, concrete, puddles and tropical plants. I romanticized the familiarity that my sisters felt when they came to Taitung once or twice a year for Chinese New Year or other special occasions, that wave of nostalgia one feels when one returns home after a long time away.

I peeked in the bedrooms. There was Ma's room; she and Ba slept separately. Strings of colored beads hung down from the door frame and formed the symbol for double happiness, a symbol of luck. She had a poster of Madonna, circa "Who's That Girl?" taped on the wall. On her vanity table, I spotted my baby picture from when I had just arrived in the United States. My sisters told me it had been there as long as they could remember.

My birth father called to me. He was on the third floor, in the room where they prayed to our ancestors. He stood before an ornate, hand-carved wood shrine featuring paintings and figurines of Guanyin and other deities. It was lit with small red lamps. Black-and-white photos of Ba's parents, Ama and Agong, hung on the wall. Ba told me the first thing we must do is *baibai,* to thank our ancestors and the gods for bringing me home safely. Jin-Xia, sister no. 3, handed me three sticks of incense and taught me to hold them with both hands and wave them three times in the air, pausing at the end. I silently gave thanks for this happy reunion. Then we placed the burning sticks in a tiny urn before the tiny golden goddess, and the smoke carried our thoughts to heaven.

FIRST, I LEARNED I had a Chinese brother that my birth parents had adopted shortly before they gave me up for adoption.

Then I learned he was fat.

Not just fat. All-caps FAT. Or "so fat," "too fat," simply "a very BIG boy." I did not even know the name of my *gege* (big brother) until I actually visited. All I knew was that my sister claimed he was about 140 kilos or 309 pounds—a scandalous size—and that I was to bring him clothing from America.

The request that I buy my big brother clothing came in the second or third letter I ever received from my Chinese family. My introduction to this family, whom I had not heard from for twenty-three years, could be summarized like this: Hello Mei-Ling. We are your birth family. We missed you. Please come back to Taiwan. And, oh, yes, please buy clothing for your fat brother.

Such a brash request might seem appalling, but my birth family has no filter. In their eyes, there was no shame in calling a brother fat or asking me—the long-lost daughter whom they gave up—to buy something for the boy they adopted and kept instead, just like there was nothing wrong with asking me how much I and my parents make and how much I spend on my apartment. But I knew the Chinese could be shockingly forward. If someone felt you were too fat, too skinny, too ugly, too small, too tall, he or she would have no qualms about telling you. My friend Marsha's mom used to chant "Tall nose, pretty girl," to her in Cantonese while pinching gently the bridge of her daughter's nose.

I went with my six-foot-four boyfriend to the Big and Tall shop and the Target store in St. Louis, and we picked through the extra-large clothing. I remember the amused look on Monte's face as he held up a pair of size XXL gray sweatpants that could stretch his entire arm span.

"This *has* to fit him," he said.

Nian-Zu was the boy that they adopted, hoping that he would

marry and have children and continue the family name. My parents and grandmother spoiled him, my sisters said. Early on, he seemed to be everything they wanted him to be.

Then he came down with a high fever. After that, my family claimed, he grew mentally slow, while his sisters were agile and smart. He grew chubby, while the girls were shapely and pretty. Our brother dropped out of school.

Now he was an adult, unmarried, and living at home, while my sisters were all educated and working. Nian-Zu often stayed in his room, mostly watching television for long periods of time, often action movies. When I met Nian-Zu in 1997, he had just gotten a job at the local fruit and vegetable market, loading and weighing winter melons, pineapples, and eggplant. He still did not know he was adopted. They might openly celebrate my return, but telling Nian-Zu about his history was not an option. Ma later said she would rather kill herself than have Older Brother find out that he was not their biological child.

Nian-Zu had waited in Taitung, while the rest of the family had gone to Taipei for my arrival. No one told me why, but I supposed my brother might have stayed in Taitung because he had to work. Or maybe he was too big to fit comfortably on a Taiwanese plane. Or maybe he didn't want to travel. But he was waiting in my parents' living room when all of us came home.

He was big, I thought, but his size wasn't that unusual to someone who had grown up with American standards of obesity. His body was large and pillowy, the folds of his tummy showing through his thin red T-shirt. He had a square head, hair that was matted down with sweat, and a warm, wide grin. He reached for me and I reluctantly succumbed to his sloppy, heartfelt hug. I noted with some shame my own reticence in returning his welcome with the passion I had embraced my sisters. Nian-Zu tried to hug his other sisters, but they also seemed to pull away, embarrassed.

Nian-Zu tried to speak to me, but I didn't understand. He spoke no English, and my Chinese was hopeless. He pulled a gift out of his pocket, a jade pendant with a monkey carved on it, a symbol of intelligence and success. It hung from a red string.

I thanked him, "*Xiexie,*" and gave him the clothing I bought him.

Later, when the family sat down to eat, the sisters translated for Ba.

"The clothes don't fit; next time you have to bring more," they said.

I stared at them, amazed, a bit taken aback. *Who was this guy?* The conversation moved on, this time to the fact that Ba was thinking about arranging a marriage—or even buying a bride for Nian-Zu—provoking a shower of loud protests from his daughters.

"You are so old-fashioned. That's ridiculous," they told our father.

He snapped back, "No it isn't!"

That evening, my third or fourth in Taiwan, was long: endless toasts and constant eating. Nian-Zu wandered in and out of the fray, rather quietly compared with my sisters, who talked, laughed, and carried on. Our brother did not even eat at the table with the rounds of family who pulled up to gorge and then retired before another round began. I later asked Min-Wei why he didn't eat with us. My younger sister's answer was simply a long, surprised pause: she had never noted his absence before.

By 10 p.m. I was beat. I was tired of the talking and of not understanding, of being bossed around, of being on display, and of constantly being photographed as if I were a baby learning to walk. I had grown up with only two younger brothers, who were still unmarried, and having several Chinese siblings, brothers-in-law, and nephews and nieces wore me out. Exhaustion and irritation were quickly replacing joy and intrigue. I could not remain open-minded and sweet without rest. I needed to escape the noise so common to my birth family. I excused myself, saying I was tired. I slipped on my pajamas and lay on a hard bed, my stomach stuffed. I breathed deeply, listening to the game of mahjong being played downstairs, the sound carrying up to my room on waves of shrieking laughter.

Write. I need to write. Release. Relax.

I reached over and grabbed my journal, flipped over on my belly, and started to write.

Suddenly, the door flew open.

There was Nian Zu.

"Get out! Go away!" I yelled, as I tried to cover myself. My sleepwear was not too sexy or revealing, but this "brother" was a stranger.

"Get out!"

He didn't understand. He was standing there, smiling a big, silly, oblivious grin. He had crammed his body into the clothes I had bought him. The bottom of the polo shirt was riding up over his stomach, which was bulging out of his pants. He rested his hands on his hips and stood very straight with his legs spread wide.

"Sank you vely much!" he said, then closed the door and marched back to his room, as pleased as he could be.

MAUREEN AND I spent three days in Taitung. We had little time alone, and when we did, we were dead tired. We got along well, but the family just sucked up all of our energy. That was okay, though. Maureen understood that this experience was between my birth family and me, and she seemed happy to be a part of it. Meanwhile, they had a hard time understanding that Maureen had not actually been a part of my life until very recently. They kept asking us questions about each other that we could not answer.

Ba drove us around, showing me off and showing off his city One morning he wrested Jin-Zhi and me out of our sleep and forced us to go with him into town, presumably because his friends would be there. We accompanied Ma to the vegetable market, where she introduced me to the vendors, friends of hers. The sisters took turns taking me to the beach, the mountains, temples, parks, and hot springs. We also toured St. Mary's Hospital. Sister Gertrude, who had been Maureen's contact at the hospital and who had arranged the adoption of our youngest sister, led us on a tour. I met some of the nurses who had spoiled and fattened me. I saw the green surgery room where I was born. Sister Gertrude introduced me to nurses and patients and told them our story.

Unbeknownst to me, my sisters were livid. They pulled Sisters Maureen and Gertrude aside and asked them not to tell people this story. They were embarrassed that my parents had given me up. It was nothing to brag about, they said.

I WAS MORE than ready to leave Taitung after a few days. I was exhausted and feeling a little frustrated. Tougher questions had begun to nag at me. I still knew so little about my ancestry, my parents and sisters' real lives. The language and cultural barrier seemed to grow minute by minute. I spent barely any time alone with my mother. Even when I did, I could only pat her hand, give her flowers or a kiss on the cheek. All these strong personalities conflicted, too. I knew there was bickering going on, though sometimes I couldn't tell if it was real fighting or their normal manner of animated, agitated speech. I caught a cold, and my throat began to ache.

I tried to hide my relief when I said good-bye to my birth

parents and headed back to Taipei with my sisters. My parents stayed in Taitung because during the upcoming holiday of Ching Ming, they had to sweep the graves of our ancestors. They told me many times that they hoped I would come back, maybe every year if I could.

"I will try," I said, doubtful.

At the airport, Ba told me for the umpteenth time that he hoped I could find Mei-Hui, our Swiss sister, and bring her back.

"I'll do my best," I said.

Ma stood nearby as Ba waved frantically. I could see his hand flailing in the air above the crowds as my sisters and I disappeared into the airport.

IT RAINED ON my final full day in Taiwan. The fog hung on the mountains, and the bright colors of the temples and pagodas seemed gray. On the way to the airport in Jin-Xia's car, we listened to an American Country Top 40 broadcast from an English-speaking station.

The twang of a Travis Tritt song somehow reminded me of the times I felt like an outsider in America, growing up. We went through the motions of the day, a trip to Tanshui Park and another unbelievable dinner at a Cantonese restaurant. After we ate, second sister, Jin-Qiong, had to return to Kaohsiung. As the taxi arrived to pick her up, she began to cry.

"I will miss you," she sobbed, triggering my tears. The others began to cry, too. Head down and whimpering, she quickly jumped into the cab and drove away. Jin-Zhi put her arms around me. I felt an intense bond with these women, and I feared that once I left, it might disappear.

"We'll see each other again, when you come back next year," she said. We climbed into two cars. In the other car, my sisters tearfully grilled Maureen.

"How does she feel about all this?" they asked. "How does she feel about the fact that our parents adopted a boy and gave her away?"

"I'm not sure," Maureen told them. In fact, I was not sure, either. During that whirlwind week, I didn't have time to digest the immensity of what was happening. That would take months, even years. I still felt as if I would wake up at any moment.

Late that night, around 11 p.m., my sisters took me and Maureen shopping, by force.

"For what?" I asked. "At this hour?" They didn't answer. They put me on the back of a moped and switched to Taiwanese so that even Maureen could not understand what they were conspiring. We sped through the streets of Taipei, passing darkened Buddhist temples and closed shops and restaurants. We stopped in front of a small jewelry store, where 24-karat gold necklaces, rings, and bracelets gleamed under harsh lights.

We were to pick my wedding jewelry. I stood there, helpless, while three of my sisters picked out two bracelets, a ring, and two necklaces. I did not want them to spend this kind of money on me.

"No! No! I don't want!" Talking to them all week had reduced my English to fragments.

They didn't listen; they just hovered over the jewelry case, pointing and picking.

They held pieces out for me to see. Exasperated, I kept protesting, paying little attention to what they were showing me.

"Ba does this for his daughters. All of us," said Jin-Hong. I soon had a full set of wedding jewelry. I took home a red plastic oval full of gold.

OUR GOOD-BYE THE next morning was hasty. We were running late, as usual. At the airport terminal entrance, I hurriedly hugged everyone, while my six-year-old niece clung to my waist. My sisters were still waving, taking pictures, and filming until Maureen and I were out of sight.

I was relieved to be on the plane. I was worn out and wanted to go home. Maureen and I quietly chatted and joked about the unbelievable visit. Meanwhile, I opened the package of wedding jewelry that my sisters had forced on me. I was so distraught at the store that I hadn't bothered to examine the actual booty. The only thing I remembered was that they had given me a bracelet made of twelve tiny gold circles, each engraved with an animal from the Chinese zodiac.

"Pretty!" they had said. "You like?"

"Yes, pretty," I said. "But I don't want."

"You are Ox. We buy for match."

Now, on the plane, Maureen and I inspected the results. The bracelet was exquisite, and the gang was all there: Dog, Pig, Rooster, Dragon, Sheep, Horse, Rabbit, Snake, Monkey, Rat, Tiger, and my sign, Ox. My sisters had followed the same theme when selecting most of my other pieces. They had chosen a thick gold chain with a circular charm engraved with the character for ox on one side and a picture of an ox on the other. I looked closer.

"That isn't an ox," I said. In fact, it was a galloping cartoon milk cow, with udders and a cowbell. Maureen agreed, laughing, too. It was a cow; the character for ox and cow is the same in Chinese.

Oh God. I better check the ring.

I looked closer.

I imagined a lovely wedding portrait, slightly out of focus except for the hands of the newlyweds. My husband's long fingers, simply adorned with a gold band, gently clasping my manicured hand. And on my delicately placed ring finger sits a puffy, golden cow, with stubs for horns.

8

MEIMEI

As soon as I returned home, I dutifully did what my birth father asked. I found our youngest sister, our *meimei*.

She was surprisingly easy to locate. I simply wrote to the nuns at St. Mary's Hospital that still kept in touch with the man who had arranged her adoption, and he contacted her. Her name was not Mei-Hui, but Irene Hofmann. The nuns told me that she wasn't sure about communicating with our birth parents just yet, but she was open to hearing from me. They gave me her address in Switzerland.

So two weeks after I returned from Taiwan, on April 21, 1997, I wrote to Irene.

"I am not sure how to begin this letter—everything and anything I could possibly write sounds strange, too awkward. So I'll get right to the point. I am your birth sister, Mei-Ling Hopgood."

In eight short paragraphs, I told her about my family, where I went to school, what I did for a living, and a brief summary of all that had transpired in the past three months. I told her about our parents, sisters, and brother, and my visit to Taiwan.

I know that this is intense stuff. And perhaps it is overwhelming. I understand perfectly. But these people are good people and have no intention of interfering with your life.

I think Ma and Ba would, at least, like to hear from you again. To know you are happy. To know you are well. They mean no imposition on your family. They know who your "real" parents are and how important they are in your life. And they respect that.

I do, too. And like I said I truly can imagine how this must feel! But I would love to hear from you — to find out who you are and what you like to do and what you do! A typical journalist! Please consider sending me a note. And ask me any questions you wish to know. Be as blunt or as straightforward as you want (I think it's in our genes). And if you feel like this is too much, you can say "back off" without hurting me.

Again, I understand. But I hope you will get in touch with me. And we'll take it from there! Love, Your sister Mei-Ling

Irene wrote me back immediately.

Dear Mei-Ling,

I hope you received my postcard. However, anyway, thanks a lot for your letter. As I wrote, I also wanted to find out your address. Maybe it was telepathy. Then I got your letter a short time later. It's quite difficult for me to write this letter in English. It wouldn't be easy even in my mother tongue, German.

Irene told me that the nuns at St. Mary's had passed on the news that we were getting together in Taiwan, but she found out too late to join us.

She went on to tell me that she was preparing for English exams and told me a little bit about her life in Switzerland. She grew up in Zug, a canton between Zurich and Lucerne. She was twenty years old and lived in the one-room flat on the ground floor of her parents' home. Her brother, Denis, was from Taiwan, too. She worked in a bank.

"Don't think that everyone in Switzerland works in a bank," she warned, jokingly. "A lot of people think of banks, cheese, and mountains if they hear Switzerland."

She mentioned that she wanted to study English, and at first she had considered England or Australia, but now that she had heard from me, she was considering America. She asked me more about my life and my hobbies. She told me that she liked to snowboard, hang out with friends, take vacations, and listen to music.

"A bit of a strange letter, I think," Irene finished. She said it was not so easy to write "the first letter to my true sister."

"Nevertheless," she continued, "I hope you understand most of it and you'll write me again! Love, Your Irene."

IRENE HAD BEEN BORN in August 1976, three years after me. Ba had already made arrangements to give her up if she was a girl. Still, Ma did not want to give her away, partly because she had been born in the celebrated Year of the Dragon, the most potent and promising of the twelve Chinese signs. Dragons could bring fortune and success. Ma thought the family needed such a child, and despite their promise to a foreign couple, she tried to keep Irene. Ba, not wanting to lose face, insisted on moving forward. He took Irene back to the hospital, where she stayed while the Swiss family made arrangements to come and adopt her.

About six months later, Monika and Othmar Hofmann, who were age twenty-eight and thirty-one, respectively, came to Taitung to pick her up. They made the trip a family holiday of sorts; a few of Othmar's siblings tagged along, too. They met Ma and Ba in a brief and emotional meeting at the house. Jin-Hong remembers crying along with Ma as she bathed Irene on that final day.

Ba tried to convince the Hofmanns to take Min-Wei, who was not even two. The Hofmanns declined, in part because they already had arranged to adopt a little boy in Taipei. The couple took their new children and returned to Europe.

After Irene, Ba wanted to try to have more children, and Ma, only thirty-three, was not too old to keep trying. Yet she was afraid that they would have another girl, and once again they would just give the child away. She feared the vicious cycle of abandonment would continue in the quest for something that might never be. So this time Ma said no, and she ended her childbearing years feeling like a failed mother and wife. And so my birth father began to look elsewhere for what he wanted.

THE FIRST EXCHANGES between Irene and me felt casual and breezy, as if we were merely international pen pals who had just been assigned to each other in class. Her extreme modesty aside, Irene's English was impressive—she spoke four languages, including her native Swiss German (as well as high German) and some French and Italian—and her handwriting was impeccable, with each letter perfectly sculpted, as if penned by a professional calligrapher. Irene told me that, like me, she had never thought much of our biological parents or family, though unlike me, she knew where they were and how to contact them. Our family had sent her some dried pineapples once in the mail. Irene told me that the man who had arranged her adoption, a former priest, had told her about me when he told her about our reunion in Taiwan.

She told me about school and the latest movies she had seen—*Speed II, My Best Friend's Wedding.* She said she shared my love for Chinese food, and food in general. I told her about my recent trips to Memphis, Los Angeles, and Mexico.

"You are a lucky girl, traveling around all the time," she wrote on September 1, 1997. I thought Irene traveled even more: Valle di Verzasca in the canton of Ticino and other spots in Switzerland, Milan, London. She sent me postcards from Vienna and Kos, Greece. To me, she lived an exciting, European lifestyle.

Early on, Irene sent a picture of herself, and even though I didn't think we looked much alike, I saw tiny bits of me in her. She was in Greece with a friend. She had short hair, a round face, and a dimpled smile, like many of our sisters have. She was wearing a white tank top that highlighted her tanned skin. She was adorable and petite (Irene described herself as 1.55 meters or about five feet tall; I'm only two inches taller) and was standing next to a very tall, white friend who had to bend down to fit in the frame with her. It reminded me of how so many of my American friends tower over me.

THE TOWN WHERE Irene grew up seems, like so many places in Switzerland, almost too idyllic to be real. In 2007 more than 103,000 people lived in the breathtaking region that embraces two crystalline lakes, Zug and Aegeri, and sits at the foot of Zugerberg. On clear days, the surrounding mountains, picturesque town, and Alpine homes reflect mirror-perfect in the lakes' surface. Hünenberg is one of eleven communities in the canton of Zug. Downtown Zug is divided into two parts, the Old Town with cobblestone walkways and medieval churches and the ultramodern office area where multinational companies have flocked to take advantage of the town's low tax rates. Zug is among the richest areas in Switzerland, a "magnet for the wealthy," as the BBC once wrote, though Irene's family was middle class. Irene told me her father, Othmar, worked as the head of the construction division in the municipality of Hünenberg, and her mother, Monika, worked part time as an accountant.

Irene grew up in a pretty four-bedroom home that her father designed with a pitched roof on a winding street called Dersbachstrasse, not far from Lake Zug. The front yard was often garnished with brilliant red geraniums. They had a swing set, a tree that the kids loved to climb, and a huge garden in the backyard where they grew their own vegetables and fruits, including beans, potatoes, cucumbers, berries, and figs. From the back of the house, they had a marvelous lake view. Her childhood was happy and simple. Her mom loved to cook and made almost everything from scratch. Their neighborhood was full of kids their age, and they usually went on a vacation during the summer (to the beach, usually Italy) and winter (skiing at a small resort). Often their many aunts, uncles, and cousins came along. They also hiked in the mountains with their extended family.

I thought Switzerland must have been an incredible, intoxicating place to live, surrounded by such pristine physical beauty: the brilliant purple and pink summer flowers, the rolling green countryside, the snowy alpine peaks, the glittering lakes and castlelike homes. The people seemed polite and well put-together. Drivers actually stop their cars when they see you want to cross the road; pedestrians always have the right of way. The air is suspiciously crisp, and views are simply otherworldly, especially to someone who grew up in a pretty nondescript suburb of Detroit. When I visited Irene in later years, I couldn't help but comment over and over again how "clean" Switzerland was.

Irene and I got a kick out of comparing the things we had in common. We loved the same hockey player: Detroit Red Wing Steve Yzerman. We wore the same furrowed expression when we lost something and the same anguished, angry look when we were hungry. We both had remarkably prehensile toes. We viewed our Chinese family and our background with similar distance and ambivalence.

We also had identical insecurities growing up. Irene was sweet, thoughtful, and had lots of friends, but though she was well-loved she also said she felt different. The Swiss population is mostly Anglo-Saxon, more so than where I grew up. In 2007 about two-thirds of the population were of German descent, 18 percent were French, and 10 percent were Italian. Irene's family is quintessentially Swiss; many of her relatives are tall, pale, and have the piercingly blue eyes of her father. Irene, too, longed to be more round-eyed and taller. Sometimes Swiss would assume she was a foreigner and speak to her in high German—Swiss speak a unique local dialect.

If someone did not like her, she wondered if it was because of who she was or what she looked like.

"I could never tell which answer would have hurt more," she told me.

While Americans might be known for being talkative, outgoing, and sometimes superficial, the Swiss can be reserved and conservative, Irene said. Her parents were caring but did not show their feelings much, which bothered her because she tended to be more emotional. She was closest to her mom, a peacemaker of sorts when Irene and her father bumped heads. The family didn't talk about her or her brother's adoption much, and she didn't ask. Actually, I would become the first person with whom she would discuss the feeling of "being different."

Irene was only twenty years old when we first began corresponding. I wondered to myself what I would have done had I been just three years younger when all this happened to me. I would have been a sophomore at the University of Missouri and in the middle of my own Asian American identity crisis. I don't think I would have been ready, although who knows if you can ever be ready for something as big as this. I wanted to ease Irene into the whole experience. From the get-go, I behaved like an overprotective big sister. She may have found our family on her own eventually, but I felt largely responsible for "bringing her back." When Irene said that she and her mother would join my American family and me on a trip to Taiwan in 1998—her father showed no interest in going, though her mom thought it was very important that she accompany her daughter—I tried to prepare her and my birth family the best that I could. I explained to her that our family could be shockingly blunt and quite pushy, without meaning any harm. I also had to remind my birth family over and over again not to refer to Irene as Mei-Hui, a name she has never used. I tried to shelter Irene from the inevitable and constant confusion in Taiwan over our travel plans; at the last minute they tried to get us all to change our travel dates, for example. I had adapted quickly to the strong personalities in our family but didn't know how Irene would react. It all could easily be suffocating, and I wanted our *meimei*'s landing to be as smooth as possible.

Meanwhile, my other younger sister, Min-Wei, was preparing to study English in the United States, an idea Irene was entertaining as well. I eagerly helped my younger sisters dig up information on study-abroad programs and invited them to stay with me. Min-Wei decided to go to California first, and then visit St. Louis for a couple months. Then, we would return to Taiwan together, where we would all be reunited—Irene and her mother, my American parents and brothers, and our biological family—in a big, loud Chinese New Year celebration in the Year of the Tiger.

I was going for it, all of it. It was as if I had all but forgotten how tiring my first Taiwan trip had been, and any warning signs and doubts that had crept momentarily into my head. I was charging forward, caught up in the newness and excitement. Sisterhood swept me away. I was so focused on getting to know my sisters and finding out the next juicy bite of information that I didn't think much about how my inquiries could impact my family or my own sense of self. Blindly, I threw my arms wide open to them, asking for more, more, more.

9

THROUGH THE LOOKING GLASS

I picture my younger sister Min-Wei as a little girl, crouched down, almost holding her breath out of pure excitement.

It is Taitung, circa 1980. She listens for her brother's heavy footfalls and stifles a giggle by pressing her hands over her mouth. The cornstalks hover high over her head, and dried husks crackle beneath her feet.

Min-Wei has memorized the fields of Taitung but not by laboring in them alongside her mother, father, and sisters. She and her older brother spend much more time playing in the rows of vegetables than working in them. Everyone else is too busy to pay much attention to what the youngest Wang children are doing. They run wild in the hot summer sun, playing games, chasing chickens, faces brown and flushed. I imagine her dark brown eyes sparkling with mischief as she crouches low, ready to jump out. She is a ball of fun and humor—and always will be—but she is also tough as nails, this seventh daughter. She will beat up any kid who picks on her big brother, who is two years older than she is, but slow and awkward, an easy target for teasing classmates. Her fists clench into pale balls instantly whenever she hears her brother's plaintive and frequent protests—*Stop it!*—from afar. She always comes running to his aid.

This forcefulness, this simmering rage will explode during her adolescence, when her parents' relationship gets so bad she cannot bear it. Min-Wei will rebel with the force of a giant against her father's old-fashioned ways. Unlike her older, more disciplined sisters, she will not study her Chinese characters. She will sulk instead of smile. She will hang around the wrong kids. She will run away more than once. Her grandmother, her parents, and even her older sisters will slap her. She will long for a different fate, and sometimes she will even think about the sister she knows she has in America. She will wonder what would have happened if only she, too, had escaped.

But for now, her spirit is unchecked, and she is shrieking with joy as she races down row after row of corn.

MIN-WEI HUNG BACK on the leather sofa and watched while our older sisters fussed over me during my first visit to Taiwan. Having grown up the youngest in a family of such forceful personalities, she knew there was no point in forcing her way into the mix. She chose instead to play cards with our brothers-in-law, glancing over, smiling, waiting for the right time to get to know me. I instantly liked her.

At that time, most of our older sisters had rather short, conservative haircuts, and Min-Wei wore hers long, with red highlights. She was more slender than the rest of us, though she liked to show off what she did have by wearing short skirts and high heels. She had full lips and olive-colored skin, like me; my other sisters were milky pale. She and I had the same peculiar habit of rubbing our itchy faces from to chin to forehead, vigorously and over and over, with our open palms. Her eyes were more slanted than mine, sexy and almost sleepy looking; yet when she posed for pictures, she opened her eyes wide so they'd appear bigger (something I've also been known to do) and sometimes looked surprised or amazed in pictures.

Min-Wei was younger than me by only eleven months and two weeks, but my family still treated her like a kid, the rebellious one who didn't go to college, who floated from job to job and who dated a foreigner. Yet I sensed she was a kindred spirit, much more inclined to be independent, open-minded, and enjoy the kind of fun (getting dolled up, going out, dancing, and so on) that I enjoyed. I knew we would get along well, even though during my first visit to Taiwan, we didn't talk much because of her limited English and my next-to-nothing Chinese. We mostly related to each other nonverbally: speeding around on her moped, strutting down the street hand in hand, feeding each other. When she told me she was coming to study English in the United States, I was excited, welcoming the chance to get to know her away from the prying eyes of our family.

MONTE AND I PICKED Min-Wei up from the Lambert airport in St. Louis in November. Clad in Levi's overalls and very high-soled tennis shoes, she strutted down the boarding ramp and threw her arms wide when she saw us. She had just finished a month of study in the Los Angeles area and she looked like a girl from Southern Cali.

"Helllllloooooooooo!" Min-Wei called out, a huge grin spreading across her face.

"*Ni chi baole ma?*" I asked, like a good Chinese sister. Have you eaten?

"No, but you are my food!" she said.

ST. LOUIS SEEMED ESPECIALLY cold during winter 1997, perhaps because I was seeing it through my sister's eyes. It snowed several times, to Min-Wei's delight; she had never seen snow before. We bundled up in hats and gloves and threw snow-balls at each other in front of a Taco Bell in St. Louis and tried to piece together a snowman. Min-Wei often ended up wearing mittens and a scarf in my house, even though I kept the heat at around seventy degrees Fahrenheit.

Min-Wei enthusiastically adapted as I tried to expose her to as much of midwestern life as I could in a few months time. We ate out often, and I took her to parks, museums, movies, and clubs. We went to see Chuck Berry play in the basement of a local club called Blueberry Hill (after which she insisted that Monte and I teach her the words to the song "My Ding-a-Ling"). We threw a party, and she and I frantically cooked for hours beforehand; she made a giant batch of fried rice, and I made taquitos. We took her to Chicago one frigid weekend, one of the coldest I've spent in my entire life, when the chill off Lake Michigan cut right through our coats and into our bones. We stuck it out for her, though, shopping along Michigan Avenue, watching the dolphin show at Shedd Aquarium, and eating deep-dish pizza. My favorite times were late at night or on long drives, when we would just talk about our lives.

Min-Wei told me that Ba and Ma tried to give her away more than once when she was a baby. One time, Ba found a Taiwanese couple who wanted a child, and the couple came to visit her when she was weeks old. But those potential parents saw something troublesome in her aura. People born in the Year of the Tiger are said to be powerful and sensitive, but also hot-tempered and strong-willed, and those were not desirable traits for a daughter. The couple decided not to take her. Irene's parents also declined to adopt her. So Min-Wei stayed.

Ma had been glad to keep her. She was spared the pain of los-ing another child, for now. She could nurse her and care for her and do all the things she could not do for me. Yet Min-Wei said she felt lost in the jumble of our family. Everyone was always too busy to pay much attention to what she was doing, how she was developing, if she was studying, if she was happy. Ma and Ba didn't even bother to name her themselves. They allowed our fourth sister, Jin-Xia, who was only six, to choose.

Mei-Fen, Jin-Xia declared, liking the sound. *Mei,* as in Mei-Ling, means plum blossom; *Fen* sounds like the word for noodle. One phonetic translation of Mei-Fen literally means "no points."

Later, when Min-Wei was a troublesome teenager, Ba took her to an astrologer to get her a new name, which he hoped would tame her. That was how she came to be Min-Wei, which means "sharp." Ba sent her to live with our uncle in Singapore, hoping to straighten her out, but after three months she returned to Taiwan and began studying cosmetology. That's when she began to turn her life around, she said.

The Min-Wei who visited me in St. Louis seemed carefree and happy. She threw herself into her English studies. Each day while I was at work, she attended a free language school in nearby University City or she stayed home and pored over her lessons. We practiced singing "You Are My Sunshine" dozens of times while riding in the car. She quickly picked up my habit of cursing at traffic. She especially liked idioms; she loved to repeat the St. Louis Blues hockey slogan she'd read on billboards, "YOU WANNA GO?" She used sayings such as "pay through the nose" and "under the weather" in conversation. One day, when I returned home from work, she popped out of her seat and proclaimed, "I feel like a million bucks!"

Min-Wei also was a dancer. She mixed it up all the time, in any place. We could be in a bar, at a hockey game, or in the supermarket. If she detected any bass, she would pump her shoulders, nod her head, and shake her hips. I found this amusing, because I, too, loved to dance, though I was a little bit more selective about where I did it. I took ballet, tap, and jazz lessons from ages three to sixteen. I loved learning the routines, dressing up in the costumes, red, pink, and green tutus and later funky leotards and fake tuxedos. (How excruciating my June recitals must have been for my parents and brothers, who sat through twenty or so acts of kids who just did pliés or spun slowly in a circle.) I fantasized about performing on Broadway, or becoming a Laker girl or a MTV video star, but my lack of long legs—and talent—were obvious impediments. Instead, I had to be content with shaking my stuff on the occasional girls' night out at the club. Min-Wei listened with interest as I told her about my dance lessons. She said dance, sports teams, and social clubs had been luxuries our family could not even imagine. They also didn't regularly visit the library—as my brothers and I had each week—nor did they take any extravagant family vacations.

I observed with great interest how my friends and fellow midwesterners reacted to my sister. For so many years, I had fretted over how people perceived me. Now I felt as if I was granted a special looking glass, through which I had an omniscient view on how others might see me. I was pleased to see that guys loved her. She was the belle of the ball at my newspaper's Christmas party. She wore my purple velvet dress—the same one that I'd worn at the cocktail party I'd thrown, the day I received that first bit of news about my birth family—and knee-high, black suede boots. A friend commented that she was absolutely stunning. I agreed, with pride, as if I had something to do with it. Min-Wei, like me, enjoyed the attention. A childhood friend who met her told me she was blown away by the similarity of our facial expressions, in particular how she lit up when people noticed her.

MIN-WEI AND I were driving my green Saturn, and I was about to pull onto a highway on one of our outings. I looked in my rearview mirror and started to turn left, onto the ramp. We were talking about odds and ends, what we would do that weekend.

Then Min-Wei said suddenly: "You know Ba had a lady."

"What do you mean?" I asked, glancing sideways at her.

Min-Wei watched my face, carefully, and plowed ahead with her story.

When she and Jin-Zhi were the only two left living in Taitung with our parents, Ba declared that he was bringing a woman home to live with them. This woman was obviously his lover and already had a son; apparently Ba thought she would be more likely to bear more boys. Ma was upset and angry, but she didn't stop her husband, nor did she leave. She still felt to blame for not being able to give Ba a boy. Meanwhile, he told his daughters that they were to call this woman auntie.

All my sisters were embarrassed and hurt, and they worried for their mother. It was as if their father had taken a kind of concubine into the house, and all of them knew it was wrong. But Ba didn't care what they thought. The fighting and crying were constant. Jin-Zhi couldn't stand it and left the house to live with a teacher.

My sister paused. I stared at the windshield, unsure how to react.

"How do you feel about this?" I asked.

"I hate it. I run away," she explained. Our parents went to the local Buddhist temple and prayed for her return. When Min-Wei decided to come home, Ba, Ma, and Grandmother beat her and confined her to Ma's room for two days. They forced her to crawl around the temple sixteen times to repay the gods for bringing her home. Min-Wei ran away again.

"I thought about find you," she told me. "I know I have sister live in America. I thought about find you and live with you."

I nodded. I was sister no. 6, between Min-Wei and Jin Zhi. I could have been a teenager living in that home, too. I saw in Min-Wei the shades of the person I could have been. I realized that I had been given a unique gift, one that I thought was only given to make-believe characters in novels or movies, like George Bailey in *It's a Wonderful Life*. I had been given the real-life privilege of seeing how my life could have been had I stayed in Taiwan, and that realization filled me with a confusing mix of remorse and relief.

"Our sisters not want you to know about this," she continued. "But I think you should know."

"I want to know the truth," I told her.

"I think this, too," she agreed.

"And what happened with this woman?"

"She leave sometime."

"Did she ever have a son?"

Min-Wei smirked.

"No."

MY FAMILY IN TAYLOR planned a big special Christmas get-together for Min-Wei, something we rarely did anymore. My parents took their artificial tree out of the attic and dusted off the ornaments and decorations. They invited our extended family over: Granny, aunts, uncles, cousins and their families. Before driving home to Detroit, I took Min-Wei to the mall to buy little gifts. We drank hot chocolate and listened to Christmas carols while wrapping the presents. In recent years, we'd opted to skip the holiday formalities, forgoing the present exchange and taking a nice trip or going out to eat instead, but we all wanted to give Min-Wei an American holiday welcome.

My sister immediately charmed everyone. She called my parents mother and father and teased my brothers. My dad took us all to a Red Wings hockey game—I was a huge fan—and he got a kick out of watching her boogie down to the between-play music. Min-Wei took photos of our snow-covered home and woods and the crackling fireplace.

When Min-Wei wasn't around, my parents asked if it bothered me to "share them" with her, but I felt no discomfort with my sister's easy integration into my family. I told my parents that it took some of the pressure off of me to take her places or show her new things. I could just sit and write in my journal while she chatted with my mom, for example. Over time, I might get envious, but the truth was that in a way, I felt guilty for the easy life I had had and was happy that Min-Wei could share it for a little while.

At one point, when Min-Wei was not in the room, my dad told me, "You know, Sister Maureen asked us if we wanted to adopt Min-Wei."

This caught me off guard. "Really?" I asked.

My parents explained that several months after my adoption, Maureen contacted them asking if they wanted my little sister, who had recently been born. At that time, my mom and dad had been just settling in with me. My parents had enjoyed our first summer together: bike rides, picnics, my first beach visits, and dips in the pool. We were settling in, a happy family unit. Mom and Dad considered Maureen's inquiry briefly but were reluctant to reestablish contact with my birth family. My mom said they did not want to risk that anything might happen that would complicate my adoption.

"What could have happened?" I asked Mom. She didn't answer, but I got the feeling that they did not want to give Ba and Ma the opportunity to change their minds about giving me up. My mom and dad thought it was better to stay far, far away and out of reach. So they said no to taking Min-Wei. But now that they knew her and loved her, they wondered if they should have said yes.

I told Min-Wei this, and she listened quietly.

"Interesting," was all she said. I wondered how that revelation made her feel, because she, too, was seeing what her life might have been like had she been adopted. Ba had tried over and over to give her away, but she ended up staying in Taiwan. Did seeing my life make her feel sad, angry, or even glad? She didn't say, but she didn't seem upset either. We all knew these decisions had been made long ago.

Still, I was eager to help Min-Wei, now that we did know each other. I hoped to offer her some of the education and opportunities that she never had. I saw how smart she was and thought it was not too late to uncork her untapped potential. I asked my parents if they might consider sponsoring a longer stay, if she decided to study more, and if they might help to pay for more English lessons. (I was not yet ready financially to assume that responsibility on my own.) Mom and Dad said yes without hesitation.

I told Min-Wei, and she said she would consider it.

Yet I could tell her thoughts had already begun to return to Taiwan. A lot was waiting for her there: her friends, the food, culture, styles, and language that she knew, her social life, and yes, her family. Although she was hard on our sisters and acted like she didn't need any of them, I sensed she cared for them more than she was willing to admit. Her boyfriend, Patrick, also hoped to reunite with her in Taiwan. She seemed less and less interested in going to English school, meeting new people, and being with me as the days wound down.

I watched her growing detachment with both understanding and disappointed helplessness. I thought America could be the answer for her, the place that could change her life, as it had mine, but it wasn't. As much as I wanted to help her, I knew I couldn't make her into the person I thought she could or should be. No one—Ba, Ma, our sisters—had been able to do that in all of her twenty-three years. She would always be that strong-willed girl who had toughed her way into adulthood. She was a Tiger. I knew only she would decide her destiny.

Min-Wei and I returned to Taiwan together on January 16, 1998, on a Singapore Airlines flight that had to make an emergency landing in Japan because it almost ran out of fuel. Irene and her mother and my American family would meet us a couple weeks later. As soon as Min-Wei got home to the apartment she shared with Jin-Hong's family, she was on the phone making plans with friends. She was back in her element. I knew she must have been tired of being forced to hang out with me all the time, and she didn't invite me along.

"I don't have to borrow your clothes anymore," she announced proudly.

I just smiled back and let her declare her independence.

10

CROSSCURRENTS

I was nervous and a little annoyed before Irene arrived.

Irene and her mother were hours away from Taipei and no one seemed to know what was going on—or at least I didn't know. Ma and Ba could not come because plane tickets during the busy Chinese New Year holiday were unavailable. Jin-Zhi, Min-Wei, and I arrived at the airport with nothing, no sign, no flowers, no leis. The sisters who had been in charge of those things were nowhere to be seen.

Min-Wei had tensed up, once again under the critical eyes of her older sisters. She and one sister had argued that day about wanting to move out on her own, and she had bickered with another about having to take the bus and train to the airport. Then yet another sister scolded her for telling me about their disagreements.

"Mei-Ling doesn't care if we fight," Min-Wei told them. But our older siblings weren't ready for me to see that side of the family yet.

This is sisterhood, too, I thought.

So everyone was irritable when we arrived at the airport. And when I saw that we were the only ones there, I became even more annoyed because I felt responsible for Irene. We borrowed a marker and paper and hastily made a sign with her name. Five minutes after we held up the sign, Irene and her mom walked out of customs.

Irene was dressed in a gray and black argyle sweater, jeans and boots. She wore her hair layered, falling just below her shoulders. Her eyes were sparkly, and she flashed us a dimpled smile. She spoke English with a British accent then. Her mother, Monika, was a thin white woman with short brown hair. They looked exhausted but happy.

We called out, waving and smiling.

"So nice to meet you!" we exclaimed, embracing them.

We quickly explained why our parents could not come to Taipei and relayed their apologies. We told them we would have to wait for our sisters to show up. I ran to buy them Cokes and guava juice, scowling all the way, trying to hide my frustration. After a fourteen-hour trip, they were being made to stand and wait in the airport.

Jin-Feng and Jin-Xia and their families showed up as we were walking toward the exit of the airport. They told us they had misunderstood the flight time. My anger subsided when I saw they had brought bouquets of flowers. Jin-Zhi smiled and said, "You have our temper," but I was in no mood to acknowledge it. We drove to our oldest sister's house, where we fed Irene and her mother dumplings and presented them with gifts. They were glad to be allowed to escape into one of the bedrooms. While they did, we wondered aloud what Irene thought of us. This time I was on the other side of the door.

IRENE'S FIRST VISIT to Taiwan went a lot like mine did. We ate constantly. We visited Taiwan landmarks. We took dozens of pictures of Irene and she took dozens of us. She and I talked for a long time one evening on a drive to have dinner with our uncle in Taoyuan, about boyfriends, jobs, and other daily things, but it was hard to find time alone. The freight train that is our family always managed to slam into any stolen moments together. Irene and I would get to know each other much better in later years, thanks in large part to Irene's incredible willingness and ability to travel to visit me.

After a couple days in Taipei, all of the sisters in northern Taiwan and their families caravanned down to Taitung to reunite with our parents, speeding our way through the precarious roads of the Central Mountains and driving down the coast.

Ma and Ba met Irene with hugs and tears. Ba would later present Irene with a red envelope full of crisp, new U.S. hundred-dollar bills to pay for her trip from Switzerland—despite her protests—just as he had done for me. I didn't notice any tears from Irene when she met our parents, but she got emotional when she saw Sister Gertrude, the nun who had arranged her adoption.

At first, Irene followed my cues, joining me at the table for meals, taking photos when I took them, going into the kitchen with me to watch Jin-Hong cook, but she soon found her own comfort and rhythm. She wandered from sister to sister, child to child, interacting on her own terms.

Irene seemed hard to read at first. She seemed reserved—even standoffish. We all puzzled over how she must be feeling. Later Irene would explain that she could be quiet in new situations, and this was certainly an experience she had never encountered before. She was taking everything in and felt conscious about making her mom, who did not understand English very well, feel comfortable. Irene was not an in-your-face, aggressive attention hound, like some of us; she bided her time, patiently taking things in. Sometimes it could take a while to get to know her well,

but once you did, you would find that she was warm, giving—
and quite feisty.

I continued to play the role of the protective go-between, the
filter between her and our birth family, though she never asked or
needed me to do this. It was instinct. I was afraid that she might
feel lost or offended. They persisted in calling her Mei-Hui, and
I kept telling them to stop. Ba and Ma and my sisters wondered
aloud about her health because she was shorter than the others.
They meant no harm and were being their usual blunt Chinese
selves, but I told them they should not say things like that. In
another instance, Irene gave everyone Toblerone candies as gifts,
but once we were in Taitung I caught my sisters giving them to
our uncle. I later told my sisters that what they did could have
been perceived as rude. They replied that they were trying to give
uncle the candies to thank him for driving us around, and they
thought it would be rude to ask Irene for more.

The one time I did not try to protect her was when the girls
decided to take her to buy her wedding jewelry. We were standing
in the Taitung living room, and they were telling her what they
were about to do. She, like I did, protested profusely. She looked
to me helplessly, and I giggled.

"I'm sorry, Irene," I told her. "I can't help you on this one."

"Ba does it for all his daughters," I said, repeating what Jin-
Hong once told me.

Min-Wei and a couple other sisters took her to the gold store,
and I stayed back at the house. An hour later they returned, and
Irene came up to me exasperated.

"Look at what they picked out!"

I looked and started laughing. Min-Wei's touch, no doubt.
Irene now had glimmering 24-karat-gold jewelry for a wedding
someday, including a couple of pieces that featured perfect hand
engravings of Mickey and Minnie Mouse.

MA CALLED MIN-WEI, Irene, and me into her bedroom to sit and chat.

"I painted my nails red because I was happy my daughters were coming home," she announced, and Min-Wei translated. We all smiled at her. She wanted to talk to Irene, to tell her the things that she and Ba had told me the year before. "We were poor . . . We wanted you to have a better life . . . But we were very sad to give you up." She recited these lines with more confidence this time, as if my visit had been the practice run she needed. Ma went on to explain that she didn't want to give Irene up because she had been born in the Year of the Dragon.

She shifted in the bed, rubbing her lower stomach. "I have trouble," she grumbled, "getting to the bathroom in time."

"Are you still sick?" I asked her. I knew that shortly before I met her, Ma had been treated for cervical cancer. Surgeons were able to remove the cancer, but she still suffered from pain, incontinence, and other problems.

"I am an old woman," she said. "I have had a hard life. I have cancer because I had too many children."

Irene listened quietly, internalizing all this for the first time. Min-Wei's voice was breaking, and I, too, could not hold back my tears. I excused myself. I rushed to the bathroom and started to bawl. Ma had given everything away, hoping she would be happy. She gave her body to Ba and to us and now she was left in shreds. I knew I was part of the reason that she had suffered. I had been one of her many heartbreaks, and I hated that.

THAT NIGHT JIN-ZHI and I slept with Ma, so that Irene and her mother could have a room to themselves. Once Ma was snoring next to us, I asked Jin-Zhi if the story that Min-Wei had told me, about the woman that Ba brought home, was true. Jin-Zhi was startled that I knew.

"Do not be mad at Min-Wei," I said. "I want to know."

She hesitated at first, but then she confirmed it.

"Yes, Father bring this woman and boy into the house. It is bad for Mother. She is so bad. And then I am so angry. I lock this boy in bathroom and I yell and threaten to kill him. But Father is angry at me. Things are so terrible. I run away. I cannot take it. I go to teachers house and hide. I leave Min-Wei at home. I know this is bad. I feel bad for leaving her alone. But I cannot take it. I am so angry at Father. Then Min-Wei is gone. She is lost. And I feel it is my fault, too."

I stroked her hair while she cried.

"I do not tell you because I want you to like Father," she said.

"That's okay," I said. "But why did you tell me he was a good father?"

Jin-Zhi paused, and then took a deep breath.

"Yes. Yes. He is good father," she said, "but not good husband."

She sniffled and I continued to smooth her hair in the darkness, trying to soothe the pain. At first Ba's obsession had seemed a cultural eccentricity, a belief I personally abhorred but tried not to judge. Now I was close with the sisters who lived with the memories and the psychological aftermath of our past. They were absorbing the pain for me, in a way. My desire for the truth was causing them despair, and I did not know how to offer any relief.

When the morning came, we pretended that I was not beginning to know the dirty secrets of our family. Irene and her mom were here. My parents and brothers were coming. This was a time to be happy. We all got up, ate our breakfast of rice porridge, and pretended that everything was as fine as ever.

Several of us went to the Taitung airport to meet my American family. They were coming from Taipei, where they had been shuttled around for a day by my uncle, Ba's younger brother.

"Hello, Mother!" Min-Wei called, waving. My little sister was animated again, friendly and smiley. My mom spotted Min-Wei and she opened her arms wide to hug us. My parents looked a bit weary, but the strange, intoxicating newness of everything was powering us all through.

MY BIRTH PARENTS' large living room is like an echo chamber. The walls are made of cement and the floor is acrylic tile. Sound multiplies in every room. One joyous shriek of a nephew bounces outward and upward through the adjacent dining room and into the kitchen, up the stairwells and through the bedrooms, up the second staircase to the room where Buddha and our ancestors hold vigil and out onto the roof. Put twenty-five people in that living room, including my dad, whose voice could bust holes in your eardrums, add a few mahjong games and a dozen shrieking kids, and you have our Chinese New Year 1998.

Ma and sister Jin-Hong manned the kitchen and pumped out dish after dish: fish, cabbage, carrots and garlic, dumplings, sautéed pork, bitter melon. We sat around the table and shoveled food into our mouths with chopsticks, then went back into the living room to rest before the next round. Both my mom and Irene's mom were astounded at the amount of food served and eaten.

We exchanged many gifts. My dad, a former high school art teacher, loved to create things, and had designed everything from my adoption announcements to the wood carving that greeted visitors at our home. For this occasion he had ordered customized T-shirts. He hand-wrote words in dramatic angles to simulate strokes of Chinese calligraphy, and sketched his own tiger. HOPGOODS IN TAIWAN, the bright red shirts said, YEAR OF THE TIGER 1998. He wrapped each shirt in red tissue paper. I watched him handing the packages to each member of my birth family.

My sisters and little nephews and nieces examined them curiously. I felt a swell of both pride and a bit of embarrassment. Wasn't this a little cheesy? But Ba immediately went to his bedroom and changed into his T-shirt, and my brothers-in-law wore them over their clothes. My parents gave Ba a silver wind chime with a tiger on it, and Mom gave Ma a necklace and locket with my baby picture inside. Ba presented both my parents with gold rings. I felt amused watching Ba boss my dad around; not many people could tell Rollie Hopgood what to do.

My mothers sat in the hardwood chairs against the wall, leaning into each other, always touching. Two of my sisters hovered over them, acting as translators. I caught snippets of the conversation. "Thank you for caring for Mei-Ling . . . No, thank you for Mei-Ling . . . No, thank you . . ." My birth mother kept patting and stroking my mom's hand. My mom observed that I had my birth mother's petite fingers, which were wrinkled from the Taiwan sun. Mom was meticulous about caring for her nails, which were always trimmed and polished.

My young niece and nephew were scared to death of my mom and her bright blue eyes and "yellow" hair. They would peek around the sofa at her, and when my sisters tried to force them to pay proper respects they would whimper and cry. My big brother, the one that my birth family adopted, kept trying to hug and kid around with my American brothers, who good-naturedly endured his brusque bantering even though they had no idea what he was saying. Irene played with our nieces and nephews. The family lit firecrackers and burned fake money for our ancestors to spend in heaven.

I flitted from person to person, though I checked often on my parents, who seemed to be having a ball. At one point, when the chatter, the laughing, and the squealing seemed to be at its peak,

I sat down alone in a chair off to the side, overwhelmed, trying to take in the madness: the children playing chase; Ba putting his arm around my dad; Mom holding Ma's hand; my sisters sharing Chinese star fruit with their kids and my brothers.

My God, I thought. *Everyone, every person, every movement— all the chaos in this room is related to me in some way.*

The noise, the smells, and the faces blurred together and seemed to crescendo into some raucous masterpiece, dissonant yet harmonic, foreign yet familiar. It all seemed so unbelievable, yet it somehow made sense. I shook my head in wonderment and could do nothing more than take a deep breath and let the cacophony crash over me.

THERE WAS NOT ENOUGH room in the Taitung house, so Ba arranged for my parents and brothers to stay in a friend's spanking-new, never-lived-in, unfurnished apartment. In fact, the whole building was empty, though the water and electricity worked. My sisters brought pillows and blankets for my family to use on the hardwood floors. My family was good-natured about the whole situation, laughing, taking it in stride. They were so exhausted that they welcomed any crash space. It was better anyway. They could have a bit of quiet and privacy, something that did not exist in my birth family's home. I had decided to stay in the house in Taitung with my sisters. My younger brother, Jung-Hoe, played mahjong with my brothers-in-law most of the night and then slept in the shrine room.

The second day went much like the first, with some touring of the city, more introductions, and lots of eating. We explored Taitung's sights. We posed for panoramic photos on the coastline, each of us balancing on our own boulder.

That night, Ba drove my parents and brothers back to the

apartment. My birth father was not a great driver. He had some trouble judging distances so he had installed two small light sticks on the front end of the car so he could see exactly where the car ended. He drove old-lady slow, at least ten miles an hour below the speed limit. The apartment building was less than a mile away, and I thought surely he could make it there and back with no trouble. Min-Wei and I waited in the living room, and Irene and her mother sat reading on the couch.

Ba burst into the house screaming his head off and waving his arms in the air. His voice was so high and frantic that he sounded like a squealing pig.

"Call the cops! Call the cops!"

I couldn't understand a word he said, but Min-Wei got a pale and panicked look on her face.

"An accident," she said. "A car accident."

My heart seemed to stop, and my head started pounding. No . . .

"What happened?" I demanded. But no one knew, and Ba would not calm down to explain. We all jumped up and ran outside and down the darkened street.

No. No. No, I chanted in my head. *This man, this crazy man didn't just harm the parents who loved and raised me? What will I do? Would this not be the worst possible outcome, the most horrible irony? That my birth family would destroy my adopted family?*

I started hyperventilating.

We reached the street corner where Ba's white car sat angled in the intersection. A group of teenagers hovered under the sallow light of the streetlamp. No Hopgoods in sight. Irene, Min-Wei, and I ran across the street to the car. Ba had been turning left and the young man hit his car, denting the fender. He had already dropped my family off. No one was hurt, but Ba continued screaming and freaking out, blaming the other driver. The boy did not have a license and Ba did not have a registered car. Irene and I peered into his darkened vehicle, then I stood there silently with my younger sisters at my side, breathing heavily.

I was so relieved. My head was spinning. My heart felt twitchy and my stomach sick. Then my sisters and our mother walked numbly back to the house.

Ma shook her head. "I don't remember the last time I moved like that," she said. Min-Wei and I laughed weakly.

Irene and her mother took their places again on the couch and tried to take up where they'd left off in their reading. Min-Wei and I sat next to each other on the couch in petrified silence. I stared at the television, at the silver sparkles on the dress of a reporter who babbled about a Chinese New Year show in Taipei. I would need hours to settle down.

MANY OF MY SISTERS had to leave the next day, to spend the rest of the holiday with the families of their husbands. As Jin-Xia said good-bye, she broke into tears.

"I'll miss you," she sobbed, and we all started crying.

Still, I was ready to go. As well as things had gone, I wanted to get my American family far away from my Chinese family, as quickly possible. I imagined that this was the feeling that my adopted parents had years ago, when they decided not to adopt Min-Wei because they were afraid to get involved with my birth family again. I felt as if I were crossing these incongruent currents of my life, pinching together two live wires that were never meant to touch, and if I held them together much longer, they might explode. Was I tempting fate? All I knew was that while I might continue to question and toy with my own serendipity, I was ready to get my mom and dad and brothers out of Taiwan.

We bade Ma and Ba good-bye and flew to Taipei. Meeting my birth family had reminded us that somewhere beyond the curtain of time existed another life, another family, and another destiny. Now my parents wanted to give the boys a chance to visit their homeland. We boarded the plane for Korea.

II

THE BIOLOGY OF ADOPTION

Seoul, 1998

The last glimmers of daylight were fading into the Han River as we landed in the city of Seoul. Giant illuminated crosses on the many churches throughout the heavily Christian city pierced the blue black sky, high above the animated billboards and sky-scrapers. Wide, high-speed roadways seemed suspended in mid-air. Mammoth digital screens, as big as or bigger than those in Times Square, lit up the downtown. During the day, you could clearly spot the giant vats of kimchee fermenting atop apartment buildings. Underground, the Koreans built an elaborate maze of walkways filled with shops, food courts, and passageways, mak-ing the insane traffic and biting cold more bearable. The city seemed exotic but much more organized and orderly than Taipei. It was indeed as its government advertised, "a clean, attractive, and global city."

My brothers craned their necks to see out of the airplane win-dow as the country they had left as children unfolded before us. I watched them closely. We had never really talked much about how we felt as adoptees. It would have been awkward, like dis-cussing our own conception. Hoon-Yung had shown little to no interest in most things Korean throughout high school and during college at the University of Michigan. Jung-Hoe had begun only recently to get to know other Korean Americans at Michigan Tech University. I hoped my brothers' experience would be positive, even if the chance that either would find out much, if anything, about his birth family was very slim. Hoon-Yung and Jung-Hoe understood this, but I couldn't help feeling nervous for them.

We arrived at the Seoul Plaza Hotel in Cheng Gu around the corner from city hall downtown. The hotel was an amazing fortress of glass and lights, a five-star affair with several restaurants and a three-level gym. We admired the marble floors and countertops in our bathroom. (*What a different experience already,* I marveled.) Jung-Hoe called his friends, exchange students he had met at college, and they took my brothers out on the town to have a few beers and Korean snacks of squid and seaweed. Mom, Dad, and I were beat to pieces from all the travel, so we stayed in.

With a great sigh of relief, I crashed on the hotel cot, a welcome luxury after sleeping for three weeks on hard beds or the floor. As I was drifting off, it occurred to me that this was the first night I had been without one of my birth family in tow during the last few months. I fell asleep immediately.

WE GOT UP EARLY on our first full day in Korea to travel by train to Incheon, the port city on the west coast of Korea where Hoon had been found. Jung-Hoe's friends, Jae Young and Mi Young, acted as our interpreters and guides.

During the hour-long train ride, people stared at our mixed group curiously, and we, in turn, inspected them. I was impressed with how tall the Koreans seemed; we spotted a few guys who topped six feet. One older woman seemed especially interested in our family and watched us for a long time before finally asking Jae Young who we were. Jae Young explained our story. The woman nodded and took my mother's hand.

"Thank you," she said. "Thank you for doing such a gracious thing to help our people."

Many of the first babies to be adopted from Korea in the 1950s and 1960s were offspring of Korean women and foreign servicemen, children who were largely rejected by the conservative and patrilineal society. American adoption agencies built strong relationships within the country and were able to place abandoned children such as my brothers in American families during socially and economically turbulent times. Westerners were adopting from Korea long before foreign adoption became popular or widely accepted; according to the U.S State Department, more American families have adopted from Korea over the last four decades than from any other foreign country.

In recent years, however, there has been considerable debate over whether Koreans should let their own be raised by outsiders. After the media aired reports that Korea was the largest exporter of babies in the world, some lawmakers, in an effort to save face, introduced legislation that would ban international adoption. The government also began various scholarship and mentoring programs and camps, to reacquaint and connect adoptees with their native land. We were visiting during a time of large-scale soul-searching in that country, my own little drama multiplied by the thousands. It seemed that the whole of Korea and its lost sons and daughters were trying to figure out where they fit in each other's lives.

WE ARRIVED IN INCHEON at around eleven o'clock in the morning.

The sprawling city sits on the Yellow Sea and is famous among war history buffs as the port where General Douglas MacArthur launched a key amphibious assault in 1950. Incheon is often thought of as an extension of Seoul because many people who live there commute to the capital for work. As soon as we arrived at the train station we asked a police officer to direct us to the Star of the Sea Orphanage. He politely obliged, and we caught a cab to the site.

The entrance was at the end of a long, icy alley. Deep red brick buildings hovered on the left, blocking the sun. To our right were the gates of the orphanage. The words STAR OF THE SEA were inscribed on white concrete at our feet and on the sign overhead.

It had been twenty-one years since Hoon-Yung had lived in this place; he had been almost two when he'd left. He studied the signs, walls, and the door cautiously and without comment. The cold whipped his cheeks rosy and tousled his thin hair. We all waited to see how he would react.

We pushed our way through the frigid air to the main building of the orphanage. It was brick, too, with steps that were made of large rocks held together by cement. I paused to take pictures, first the whole family together, then just Hoon. It was an odd portrait. We smiled touristy smiles, as though we were posing in front of any other monument or landmark, and then entered the building.

It was eerily quiet, and our footsteps echoed through the lobby. The only man we could find was the orphanage accountant. Through Mi Young, we explained why we were there. He told us that none of the other officials were there, but he graciously agreed to show us around. We walked slowly through the small complex of buildings, letting Hoon lead. The man gave us the basic facts, no more and no less. He explained that in 1983 many of the older buildings had been razed and replaced with newer facilities. A preschool was added in 1994. However, the building where Hoon stayed still remained. It was an ordinary brick building, nondescript and square. We couldn't see inside because the windows sat high, though beyond the snowy panes, we did glimpse bits and pieces of the toys that sat on the ledge inside: an elephant's ear, a red box, a doll's blonde hair. The man said he couldn't let us enter because he did not have permission, and most of the children were sleeping. There are fewer adoptions these days, domestic or international, he said. Mostly they were taking in children from broken homes. The tour lasted barely fifteen minutes.

The man could not tell us anything about Hoon-Yung's case. He didn't have access to the files and didn't know when the others would be back. He apologized for not having more information and told Hoon that he was happy to see things had worked out so well for him, that he had a good life and a good family. He shook our hands and led us out.

We returned to Seoul and visited the agency that handled the Korean end of both brothers' adoptions. Administrators at the city's social welfare agency could verify that they had limited records for the boys, but they would have to be formally requested, dug up, and sent to us later. We decided that the trip to Jung-Hoe's native Kwang Ju, 160 miles south of Seoul, would be too ambitious for our brief stay. Instead, Jung-Hoe spent the rest of the afternoon visiting schools to check out language programs. He was on track to graduate from the university in three years, and my parents were encouraging him to consider studying abroad. He wanted to come back to Korea.

We had all hoped that Hoon-Yung and Jung-Hoe might find out a little more, especially after experiencing Taiwan and my crazy, welcoming, and repenting birth family, but there were no big discoveries or breakthroughs to be made in Korea. As with many international adoption cases, the circumstances of my brothers' abandonment had always been fairly unknown, and it looked as if things might stay that way. We spent the next couple days sightseeing, eating, and meeting Jung-Hoe's friends and their families.

At first, I felt sorry for my brothers, but then I remembered how I had been happy in my little cocoon of ignorance. None of us had ever doubted the destiny that we had been given. For my brothers, it was enough to see, smell, and experience Korea. They had fun hanging out with Korean pals, eating kimchee, *kim bop,* and *bulgogi.* They gulped down shots of *soju,* a Korean rice liquor, and played Korean billiards. They got a tourist's-eye view of their homeland, and that was enough.

Hoon said that visiting the orphanage was a precious, positive experience, his first concrete link to his past, but he added, "It was not overwhelmingly emotional for me, but I had certain expectations that were basically met and not exceeded."

For Jung-Hoe, visiting Korea was monumental, improving his sense of identity, confidence, and independence. He told me that when he heard that I had contacted my family he was envious, and yearned for his "biological home," although he did have some reservations upon learning the complicated story of my family.

Jung-Hoe indeed would return to Korea to study a year later. He would go to his orphanage in Kwang Ju to see if he could dig up any more information. He would only find the papers that talked about his reserved and sweet personality and would discover that he had been found wandering the streets after a civil uprising, holding the hand of an older child. A relative? A brother? A friend? We may never know, yet these unanswered questions did not make him or Hoon any less happy or successful in their lives.

I sometimes resented people's assumption that adoptees must

automatically, deep down, feel part empty or abandoned, that we must suffer some hole in us that will never be filled because our birth parents could not or did not raise us. I know people think this. I know because psychologists and adoption experts write essays and books about it. I know because of the questions people ask ("Did you always know you were adopted?" "How did you feel about that?") as if being adopted might mean you are somehow incomplete.

I also understand that adopted parents worry a lot about this. I've talked to parents who pine and mourn for their child's birth mother and father and fret over whether their baby will despair at not being able to know or find their birth family. I know parents who fear telling their child that he or she is adopted, which is ridiculous, in my view. The longer you conceal this so-called secret, the more likely it will become toxic.

Ultimately, I think people tend to forget that on a basic level our relationships with our adopted parents are normal parent–child relationships. The only difference is how we became parent and child. We can get along great and we can hate each other. We love and fight. We can long for another fate or adore our families and never want anything else. It's not biology that defines the relationship. In fact, one might argue that adopted families start out in a better spot, as Jung-Hoe pointed out, because of all the background checks and vetting that the parents have to go through. At least they have to prove they have the means and the heartfelt desire to raise the child.

Perhaps I have an overly unsentimental, simplistic view on the subject. I've always known I was adopted. I also know that my adopted parents loved us more than anything. I think that's why my brothers and I have been able to keep our pasts in perspective. I know for other adoptees, it's a more complicated question, and they do feel a tremendous loss. After I wrote a newspaper article about my first reunion with my birth family, agencies and support groups eagerly invited me to speak on panels with other grown adoptees. I was taken aback listening to one woman talk about how betrayed she felt by her birth mother. I had never felt that way. One friend of Jung-Hoe's told me, bitterly, about meeting his Korean birth mother. She had agreed to see him in a Seoul train station. She was obviously nervous that people would see them and tried to give him money so he would not contact her again. He threw the money back in her face and angrily left.

"I hate that bitch," he told me. "I don't care."

I also know plenty of adoptees who don't even think of their birth parents, and have little or no interest in ever finding them or even visiting the place they were born. They have been offered the information and have refused. There are countless factors that influence the way we view our families, our adoptions, and ourselves—and they are the same factors that impact how other children see themselves. No one adoptee's view is more right or wrong than another's.

If I really thought about it, I didn't automatically feel a strong connection with my birth parents. I had thrown out almost carelessly the words *I love you,* but did I really mean them? I felt something, although I certainly did not care for them like I did my parents in the States. I did feel a special bond with my sisters that was growing stronger, but I was not some passive player.

I *wanted* to love them—and I wanted them to love me.

I was actively choosing to open my heart, revising my personal history and reconstructing my family. I never would have imagined that I would want to take a sledgehammer to the wall between then and now and upset the applecart of my identity. My sisters had revealed the first gnarled flaws in our family tree. (There were so many sisters with differing opinions and personalities that no secret could stay hidden for long.) I was just beginning to get to know the real people behind the happy façade. Each revelation, each visit, each conversation opened a whole new set of questions. *Who really were these people? What was it really that I missed and that I now belonged to? Who am I?*

I wanted to know the real family, not just the version that they wanted me to see. I was more interested in the complex and the difficult. I just wanted the truth. I had a journalist's curiosity, the Hopgood spirit, the anxious blood of a Wang.

"They don't want you to know about Ba," Min-Wei warned me.

To me, that kind of proclamation was practically a dare.

12

HANDMADE DUMPLINGS

I love dumplings.

I have loved them ever since my parents used to take us to Chinese and other Asian restaurants in Detroit, Toronto, Ann Arbor, and Chicago. I adore their compact efficiency, how perfect they look on the plate, the burst of hot flavor in my mouth. I eat them steamed, boiled, fried, in soups, or crispy and hot off the grill. I like them quarter-moon-shaped, or plump and doughy, or twisted up like oversized Hershey's kisses. I'll eat them filled with cabbage and carrots and pork or shrimp and mushrooms or spinach and onions. I have savored sizzling *guotie* in a home restaurant in Kinmen made by a grizzled woman who hovered over a greasy, crackling grill while her children pulled at the folds of her skirt. I have inhaled an inhuman number of *shumai, hargou,* and other types of dim sum in smudgy dining rooms in Hong Kong. My husband and I physically crave *xiaolongbao,* a perfect specimen of dumpling from eastern China that is filled with soup, as well as the meat or seafood filling, and explodes with flavor when you bite into one. Eating them in Taipei's famous Din Tai Fueng restaurant changed my life, and whenever we are in New York we are sure to order them at Joe's Shanghai. To me, dumplings are almost an obsession.

What a joy it was to have access to a family who knew how to make, buy, and eat the best dumplings. That first morning I woke in Taipei, Min-Wei was eating dripping pork dumplings from a clear plastic bag, and offered me one, winning my heart forever. Fourth sister Jin-Hong later hand-made *shuijiao,* boiled dumplings, for the entire family when we visited Taitung.

"Please teach me," I begged, and she pleasantly agreed.

Jin-Hong and Ma took me to the local market where we picked the handmade dumpling wrappers and the freshest cabbage, carrots, and pork meat. At home, my sister took me to the kitchen and led me through the steps.

First, you finely chop the pork into tiny pieces, and then the cabbage even more finely. Make sure you squeeze out the excess water from the cut vegetables and the juice from the meat; the mixture has to be as dry as possible.

Jin-Hong added a dusting of what I believe was cornstarch, though neither of us could translate that word into the other sister's language. Then she threw in some garlic. She opened the dumpling wrappers and placed one in my hand. They were light circles, floury and cool in the palm.

She placed another wrapper in her slightly cupped left hand and put a dollop of the meat-vegetable mixture in the center. She folded the wrapper in half and pinched it together at the crest and she pulled delicately and quickly at the dough, folding forward tiny waves of wrapper until she had a perfect pregnant-looking crescent. She set it on a plate and picked up another wrapper. I clumsily tried to imitate her fluid movements.

Dumpling making is often a team sport, with the entire household participating. My other sisters and even brothers-in-law gathered around the table, joking, laughing. They filled and folded their lopsided dumplings and declared, "Mine is most beautiful!"

When all the wrappers were used up, Jin-Hong showed me

how to cook the *shuijiao* just right, dropping them in a boiling wok adding a cup of cool water, waiting until the water bubbled up again and then repeating twice more. She scooped out the result in a strainer, and tossed them steaming hot on a plate. They tasted fantastic, especially with soy sauce, vinegar, and chili sauce. They disappeared in seconds.

I mentally recorded Jin-Hong's lesson and practiced it when I returned to the United States, assisted by a newly purchased Chinese cookbook. Each time, I got better and better at making them. Wherever I lived, I sought out Chinese grocery stores, hunting down the best place to buy the wrappers and fresh ingredients. I adapted the recipe to American products and cooking accessories. I bought the pork already ground, and after spending many hours using a knife to chop the cabbage into tiny pieces, I purchased a food processor. I used my sister's boiling method for a time but later switched to a bamboo steamer. That way I could make more, faster. I mixed Chinese tradition with a few modern conveniences to satisfy my American impatience.

I enjoy the ritual of making dumplings, the feel of the soft, malleable dough against my fingertips. It's therapeutic to spend an hour folding in front of the television the afternoon before a party. Sometimes I invite girlfriends over to bond over dumpling making. My dumplings are, to this day, the most popular dish at my dinner parties.

"You made these by hand?" People ask in wonder.

"Yes," I say proudly.

"Where'd you learn?"

"My sisters," I respond. And they nod approvingly, as if it must come naturally.

I HAD SPENT most of my young life trying to prove how American I was. I had wanted more than anything to disassociate myself with anything Asian. When I went away to the University of Missouri in Columbia (nicknamed Mizzou), I rushed a sorority, in which aside from the half-Asian president, I was the only minority. I wore those Greek letters big and bright on my chest like an announcement: "Look! I am American." However, among the white girls from mid-Missouri with big bows on their heads, I still felt awkward and out of place even though no one treated me that way. I stared at the other Asians on campus, noting how foreign they seemed, and felt ashamed that in my own head I was perpetuating the stereotypes I abhorred.

It wasn't until my sophomore year that I began to figure out that being different was okay, and one of the touchstone events was when I made my first Asian American friend in college.

Her name was Tisha Narimatsu, and she was in my news writing class, which she hated because she planned to go into advertising. Tisha had been born and raised in Honolulu, where more than half of the residents have some kind of Japanese, Chinese, Korean, Filipino, or other Asian blood. She was half Chinese, half Japanese, an unusual combination considering that the two ethnicities generally hated each other. The issue of race to her at Mizzou was something completely different; she had never been in the minority before. She was stunningly blunt and spoke with a slightly pidgin accent when she relaxed and stopped carefully cleaning her speech. For example, she said "da" instead of "the" and "I'm code" instead of "I'm cold." I thought she was interesting, and the perfect candidate for an Asian partner in crime after deciding out of the blue that I was ready for one. I liked that she seemed comfortable in her skin in ways I was not and pursued her friendship aggressively. I talked to her during class, asked for her number, and invited her out. I was like a kid with a crush. Tisha was used to a more polite, nonintrusive Asian style, and I scared her a little, but she went along with it. In the end, we became good friends. Mainly, we went out to parties and bars, drank a lot of Bud Light, and met guys.

One night after returning from happy hour, I made her stand in front of a mirror in my bedroom next to me so I could compare our eye shape. I was a little buzzed and wanted to see if it was true that we looked alike, as so many white folks in Columbia said. Tisha thought all this was ridiculous but humored me. I remember giggling as we stared at each other in the mirror. In fact, we did not look so alike. My eyes were bigger, more almond-shaped and slightly crooked. Hers were more even, a bit longer, shaped more like a thin slice of the moon. My nose protruded; hers was wider. I had angular eyebrows; hers were more curved.

This firsthand proof—that all Asians, in fact, do not look alike—was one in a series of discoveries that might have been obvious to Tisha, my sisters, and others but was not so apparent to me. At about the same time, I was recruited, still reluctantly, into the first and only Asian American group on campus back then. That first meeting was strange, all of us in once place. I remember nibbling the Korean cookies that someone brought and being ultra-aware of the Asian-ness of everyone in the room. I wondered what I had in common with them, besides our ancestors being from the same general continent, but I related to their tales of feeling harassed or isolated. I attended more meetings and began to forget about race: theirs and mine. I also got involved with the Asian American Journalists Association, through which I met a ton of incredibly smart and successful Asian Americans who defied the stereotypes.

By the time I graduated from college, I had figured out that I actually liked being Chinese American, but I still tried to convince people—most of all myself—that my past might have dictated what I looked like, but it would not determine who I was or would become.

Then I met my birth family and suddenly found myself trying to be Chinese.

I yearned to understand my birth parents' words with my own ears, instead of always having to rely on the labored and carefully edited translations of my sisters. I had studied Mandarin with friends and at a local Chinese school, and I listened to the tapes that my sisters gave me, but my grasp of the language was still abysmal. I read some books and saw some more movies, but I knew little about what it meant to be Chinese.

The only way to learn, I decided, was to get out of St. Louis, to slam the brakes on the quick progress I was making as a young journalist at the newspaper there. My bosses liked me, my sources trusted me, and my articles were making the front page. Yet my world had changed. The history that once seemed so irrelevant to the life I was leading in the United States was now shaping the future I envisioned for myself. The contours of the American identity that I hard worked so hard to forge were graying and morphing. I was embracing a kind of dual citizenship but was not sure yet what membership meant. What I did know was that I wanted to know more, and that meant a complete revision of my life's plan. I won a journalism fellowship to study Mandarin and Chinese history, politics, economics, and literature. My next destination: Hawaii.

TRADE WINDS. Marbled blue waters. Killer waves. Taut and tan bodies. Lots and lots of Asians, *hoppas*. Pidgin English. Incredible pan-Asian food. My friend Tisha and her Hawaii pals. Island life was in my blood, you could say, but who wouldn't want to live in Hawaii? For eight months I lived within a bike ride of my classes at the University of Hawaii and a short walk to the ocean. Aside from my real classes, I took scuba, hula, and surfing and I got to be part of the "majority," just another Asian face (until I opened my mouth and talked like a *haole*, a white person). Aside from soaking up the sun, I did in fact improve my Mandarin during those two semesters, although I finished far from fluent. I visited China and found I could strike up a low-level debate with Beijing cabbies on the significance of the tenth anniversary of the Tiananmen Square massacre and I could avoid ordering dishes at restaurant with dog or snake meat. I was making some progress, but I was a long way from figuring out how all these changes fit into my life.

LITTLE MORE THAN a year and a half had gone by since Min-Wei stayed with me in the United States. Her life had changed drastically by the time I returned to Taiwan in July 1999. Not long after she returned to Taipei she married Patrick and got pregnant. When I arrived for a visit with Monte and my brother Jung-Hoe, the couple were living with their new baby girl, Tasia, and running an English school out of their apartment.

Ba at first disapproved of Min-Wei's marriage to Patrick—whom he saw as a white foreigner who was not rich enough—and made it rudely and painfully obvious when he arrived in Taipei to meet me. When he walked into their apartment, Ba completely brushed by his daughter, ignored Patrick, and showed no interest in her baby.

"I don't care," Min-Wei said, waving it off, but I was annoyed. My own dad had not always been thrilled with my taste in boyfriends through the years, but he always treated my dates with courtesy, and above all he respected my opinion. It seemed to me that Ba selectively valued his daughters' opinions. He had wanted Min-Wei to marry some older Chinese man, who supposedly had money. It was for her own good, he said, but that wasn't what Min-Wei wanted. Ba did try in his own gruff way to welcome Monte, who had asked me to marry him only a couple weeks prior in a courtyard in Singapore. Monte and I had been dating for three years, since right around the time I made first contact with my birth family. He had been patient and tolerant, joking with the sisters who visited and putting up with incredibly early phone calls from Taiwan; my family often miscalculated or did not bother to heed the fourteen-hour time difference. In Taiwan, Monte took in stride my birth father's brusque behavior. The two men couldn't speak to each other, anyway, but at least Ba acknowledged his presence by pushing him to eat. I guessed that since I was a foreigner, Ba knew he had to accept that I would have a foreign husband. Ba knew his influence in my life was limited, but that didn't mean he did not try to impose his opinion.

MY BIRTH PARENTS had shared with me tidbits about Kinmen during previous visits, stories of my grandparents and of the war and the poverty that had dogged them. Ma and Ba were anxious for me to return so that I could meet my many aunties, uncles, cousins, and friends—or rather, so they could meet me. So this time, we went with my sister Jin-Hong.

In 1999 Kinmen still seemed suspended between China and Taiwan, communism and capitalism, war and peace. The old-style homes were magnificent with their red sloping roofs, but spanking new multilevel homes towered over them, making them seem almost shabby. The island looked and felt like a military town, in various shades of gray and khaki. Villagers selling fruit trudged past infantrymen, who stood in the shade of roadside trees and smoked Marlboros. Many of my relatives were hard country folk, with leathery skin, missing teeth, long hairs growing out of cheeks, and facial moles. (My birth father sometimes let grow a few curly and rather creepy sprouts on his chin.)

We visited Ba's ancestral home in the West Garden neighborhood where he and Ma lived during the early years of their marriage. We parked the car and walked down the narrow alleyway that led to the house. A small wooden door opened to a traditional Chinese courtyard. The space was dirty with only a few stray tools and pieces of random furniture strewn here and there. A layer of dust covered everything. A central room still held our dilapidated ancestral shrine, and we paid our respects. The rest of the house, which consisted of a few small rooms emanating from the main courtyard, was abandoned. Ba showed me a small garden area, now overgrown with weeds and vines, where he said Chinese bombs had almost killed him. Before we left West Garden, we tended the graves of Ba's parents, which were nestled in a nearby field.

During the evening we stayed in the modern house that Ba and Ma had bought, a few hundred feet from the sea. I took a walk down a newly paved road along the coast, watching the ocean pound against old gun turrets and inspecting rocks covered in shards of glass. You wouldn't risk swimming here for fear of being crushed by the surf or dashed on the wreckage left from the war.

All of this was interesting to me, but I felt little if any romantic attachment to Kinmen's rustic charm. I think my own mixed feelings about my birth parents might have clouded my opinion of the place.

As usual, I was always on display. Not only did they want to show me the war memorials, they wanted to introduce me to all the relatives they could round up. Certainly everyone was welcoming. They cooked elaborate meals and gave me improvised gifts: jewelry, cakes, pens, and clothing. Everyone wanted to toast me with the throat blistering rice liquor that Kinmen is known for. But it was tiring to be the center of so much attention, especially when I still did not understand the language. In Kinmen, the common language was Holo (Taiwanese), so despite my best efforts to learn Mandarin, I was still left out of most conversations and tired quickly of those I did recognize: where I lived, and what I did, how much I made, why I was so "black."

In Taiwan and China, being "black"—meaning tanned or darker skinned—is undesirable. Color was considered a sign that you were from a lower class, that you labored outside or had indigenous roots. My family had been poor once, but they preferred not to look like it. When my Chinese sisters came to visit me in Hawaii, they hid in the shade, slathered themselves with super-strong sunscreen, and wore hats. In sharp contrast, when Irene came to visit me in Hawaii, we loved lounging at the beach. To us, being tan meant we were healthy, vacationed, and relaxed. I liked how I looked with a little color, but for my Chinese father it was something that he had to excuse.

"She is so black because she lived in Hawaii, where she had a scholarship," he told everyone.

After hearing this refrain over and I over, I grew annoyed. Why should I make excuses for the way I look? Despite my best efforts to understand their culture, I felt like some members of my family didn't even try to understand mine.

Finally, during one dinner, when my skin color came up again, I said in Chinese, defiantly: "I like being black."

Jin-Hong glanced at me surprised but then smiled at this small retort, a flickering of protest from the American daughter. Ba and everyone else just looked at me like I was crazy and went on with their meal.

I WAS SO GLAD to have Jin-Hong in Kinmen, to be able
to devote these two short days to getting to know her a little better. I was drawn to my fourth-oldest sister, who seemed level-
headed but still fun and fairly liberal-minded. She was four years
my elder, and the other sister aside from Min-Wei that everyone
thought I resembled. She and I had the same kind of curvy body,
though she was taller and paler. She was a wonderful cook. She
tended to be more mature and responsible than Min-Wei growing
up but still did things like drink a beer once in a while.

At the time, she was married with two young children, but she
took time off from her job to accompany my parents and me to
Kinmen. Jin-Hong was used to the indiscriminate comings and
goings and last-minute decisions our parents imposed. They were
always jumping in and out of the car, running into a store to buy
vegetables or into a friend's home to say hi. She and I were often
left sitting in the car, her in the driver's seat shaking her head at
whatever was just said or done, and me watching her, confused.

Once, after Ma and Ba had said something to her in Taiwanese and exited the car, Jin-Hong looked at me, narrowing her
eyes in the rearview mirror.

"Did you understand that?"

"No," I said.

"You know what my Taiwan name, Awan, mean?" she said,
referring to the nickname that our grandmother and parents had
given her when she was born.

I shook my head no.

"My name mean 'no more girls,'" she said. I stared back at
her, watching her watching me. She didn't blink.

We have another cousin, too, she told me, who has a name
that means "wish for a boy."

I grimaced and shook my head, feeling sorry for her and my

cousin. Some Chinese families named their children after qualities one might aspire to, such as grace or justice. Mine named a daughter after an obsession. Jin-Hong seemed unmoved. That's just how our parents were. Ba had paid for her schooling, encouraged her to study, but it was she herself who managed to rise above this nickname, become a computer engineer and saleswoman, and lead a good life. She had defined who she was.

During the evening, Jin-Hong and I snuck away to the roof of our parents' home, where they had spread peanuts on the floor to dry. We sat in white plastic garden chairs and on crates and talked while we looked at the brilliantly starry sky.

My sister's marriage was on the verge of breaking up. She and her husband had married young, not long out of college. She wanted a divorce, but she told me, in Taiwan, children belonged genetically and legally to their fathers. She would have little ground to fight for custody, since her husband had not carried out any grave offense against her. If she left, she would undoubtedly lose her kids, and she couldn't bear that thought. That's why she stuck around in an unhappy situation, because fathers had more rights than mothers.

I told her in the United States the opposite was often true. She nodded sadly and stared into the night.

Society had come a long way. In Chinese cities and among the younger generations, families wanted girls as much as boys, but such a deeply engrained belief does not change and disappear even over a century. It lurks like a latent virus in laws, memories, and traditions. It surges forth when we least want to remember. Though we try, we might never escape its reach. In the end, my sister would get a divorce and give up custody of her children, although they stayed with her on the weekends.

Ba interrupted our bonding. He came upstairs barefooted and

wearing a white tank top. He stood next to me, leaning against the wall. I could tell he desperately wanted to ask me questions and bond with me.

He asked: How were my parents? How was my job? How were Irene and her family? They were friendly questions, the inquisition of an interested father. But I answered shortly. I didn't understand and didn't feel like trying. I wanted a second of peace, away from his judgment or remorse. I wanted to be with my sister. We sat in silence for several minutes.

Finally, Ba gave up and returned downstairs. Jin-Hong and I smiled at each other, almost triumphantly, and continued talking late into the night.

The next morning when we woke up, Ma scolded us.

"Bad girls," she said to Jin-Hong. "You were smoking. I saw the cigarette butts."

Jin-Hong smiled mischievously and ignored her. To my chagrin she didn't tell her that it was she who had been smoking and not me. I got the feeling that she liked the idea that Ma might think that I was a bit rebellious, too. I didn't want Ma to think I smoked but said nothing. At that moment, I preferred to be a good sister rather than a good daughter.

EACH TIME I VISITED, and each time my sisters visited me, I collected a little bit of vocabulary, history, habit, and tradition and tucked it away in my brain. I bought Chinese scrolls to decorate my house. I learned simple songs and dirty sayings. I can say "fart," "drink beer," and "make love" in Mandarin. I could sing funny little nursery rhymes. In Beijing I bargained in tiny shops for two traditional *chipao* dresses, embroidered silk with high mandarin collars and slits up the sides. I would wear those dresses on special occasions, including my wedding rehearsal dinner.

I copied some of my sisters' styles. I saw, for example, that none of my sisters wore bangs even though I'd always had them because I hated my forehead (I thought it was too high). Soon after I met the girls, however, I grew out my bangs and have not cut them since. I wore open-toed sandals and higher heels, like they did. I was proud of "looking Asian," something I couldn't have said merely five years before.

I was developing a new culture of my own, which neither set of parents had handed down to me. Certainly, I may have inherited a love for vegetables from my birth mother or a penchant for the dramatic from either one of my fathers, but the new habits and tastes I had begun to co-opt were not biologically mine nor did they grow organically from my childhood. In fact, I was becoming the Asian American that people had always assumed I was, with a culture that came with the face.

13

DADDY'S GIRL

Washington, D.C., 2000

Many of the bars and restaurants in the southeast quadrant of Pennsylvania Avenue around the corner from the House of Representatives' offices were pubby joints with names like Hawk 'n' Dove and Politiki. They served decent burgers and stiff drinks at inflated prices to congressional staff, lobbyists, and journalists after a long day on the Hill. Walls were covered with presidential paraphernalia, and floors got syrupy sticky around the close of happy hour. The bars on the House side were generally not the hot spots where high rollers with endless expense accounts schmoozed powerful legislators, but plenty of key legislative haggling went on in the booths and around the cigarette-scarred tables.

My husband and I liked this neighborhood, though mostly for its convenience. When we first moved to the area for Monte's new job with the *Washington Post,* we lived in Maryland and this was the first strip of decent night spots on the way into the district. It also was a ten-minute walk from the office where I'd eventually work and little more than a mile away from the house we'd eventually buy. But we chose to meet my parents for dinner there precisely because we thought that it had the D.C. feel that my dad liked so much. The buzz of politics was always in the air: the latest bill, the hottest up-and-comer, the most spectacular crash-and-burn.

My dad was a political junkie to the core, a loyal foot soldier for the Democratic cause. Every campaign season he filled our front yard with fluorescent signs advertising the appropriate candidates. He would walk through the door with his arms full of propaganda, and my mom would ask, "So what are we supporting today?" We kids were recruited to pass out campaign literature in the neighborhood as soon as we were tall enough to open mailboxes, buoyed by the promise of hot chocolate and doughnuts. Almost yearly we marched or rode on the floats Dad designed for the Labor Day parade in Detroit, waving our UNION, YES! signs.

My parents had come to D.C. for a national meeting of teachers union officials just before the presidential election of 2000, barely a month after Monte and I moved to the nation's capital. The four of us met at Bullfeathers, a well-known Hill bar named for President Theodore Roosevelt's favorite cuss word. My dad came straight from a business meeting and political rally and wore a large GORE 2000 campaign button on his chest. His face was flush with excitement.

The waitress noted Dad's pin and asked him who he worked for.

"Not many Democrats come in here these days," she said. Bullfeathers was one of the more Republican-leaning joints at that time.

Dad grinned, as if accepting a challenge.

"I work for the Michigan Federation of Teachers, and I'm here to support Vice President Gore," he said. "And who are you voting for?"

I cringed. This was not a conversation that I wanted to get into, especially before I could order my burger. My father was always doing this, chatting people up, telling them more than they needed to know and how they should be thinking and voting. Most people got a kick out of him, and I admired his bold ability to engage anyone in a conversation about anything. But as I got older, my father's lack of inhibition—particularly when it came to politics—mortified me. I would recoil whenever he'd launch into one of his diatribes about collective bargaining or union solidarity. I've always shared most of my dad's liberal beliefs, but politics bored me—if not repulsed me. I would debate my father, just to challenge what I thought was blind devotion to causes and leaders that did not always have the best interest of the people in mind. Today I appreciate his resolution, even his gall, and his bulldozing eyes-on-the-prize drive, which he used to get me into this country and teach me to be a strong woman. Yet at times like this—when a poor waitress was forced to admit that she was, in fact, for the other team and then had to put up with my dad's ribbing—made me want to crawl under the table.

A COUPLE MONTHS LATER, I managed to land a job with the *Dayton Daily News*, a scrappy midsized newspaper in Ohio owned by Cox Newspapers. It seemed ironic to me that I would end up in the nation's capital, immersed in my father's domain of politics and government.

I suddenly was a Washington correspondent. The title sounded so much more glamorous than the job was. To do it right, I had to give myself a crash course in parliamentary procedure and memorize the names and faces of all the Ohio representatives and senators, and the names and faces of the staffs that ran their lives. I had to dissect the Air Force Materiel Command's principal and supplementary budgets and endure long hearings on sexy topics such as the human capital crisis. I read into prefabricated statements and combed through campaign finance reports. I haggled with press secretaries over fine points such as whether the senators supported or just didn't oppose the president's most recent proposal.

Actually, it was a great job, and I did it well enough, but I never felt like I quite fit in among the ultracompetitive Washington press corps, the bureaucrats and staffers who cared more about who you worked for (and how you could help them) than who you were. I always had to restrain myself from openly jeering at the know-it-all reporters who dropped names and threw out government jargon at press conferences. The ass-kissing drove me nuts, though I did meet many genuinely good people on all sides who wanted to make a difference, and I certainly didn't mind the fantastic source lunches in restaurants such as TenPenh or Charlie Palmer.

I did have some incredible experiences: walking across the White House grounds, wandering the labyrinth of the Pentagon or the halls of Congress, talking face-to-face with some of the political figures of the day: Hillary Rodham Clinton, Donald Rumsfeld, Ted Kennedy, and President G. W. Bush. We were living in Washington on September 11, 2001, when terrorists attacked the Twin Towers and the Pentagon. I stood, eyes watering, in the still-smoldering military headquarters listening to Defense Secretary Rumsfeld vow that the United States would not bow before any threat. Those were mind-blowing days, when the country was full of anxiety, and our jobs as journalists seemed especially important. I learned more than I could have ever dreamed about the way our government and our country works.

But on slow days, I still ended up foraging through the garbage of government looking for stories. During some downtime on March 12, 2002, I let one of my more persuasive press secretaries convince me that I *had* to go to a meeting of the Senate Committee on Environment and Public Works. The senators were going to talk about the "the proposed First Responder Initiative" in President Bush's 2003 budget or, in real-people English, why Bush wasn't giving enough money to firemen, police, emergency workers, and the agencies that would have to respond to another terrorist attack or national disaster.

How the heck did I get talked into this? I thought an hour into the testimony. I sat somewhere in the middle of the hearing room in the Senate Dirksen Building. Sure, the topic was important, but it was as boring as heck. I was struggling to stay awake while the director of the Federal Emergency Management Agency talked about how he desperately needed hiring flexibility to attract and keep good employees.

My mobile rang, a no-no during a live hearing. I fumbled around in my purse and quickly glanced at the number, which rang in "private." I shut off the phone, figuring whatever it was, it could wait. The hearing ended after another hour. I trudged back to the office, my arms full of witness testimony. I felt dismayed that I had wasted those two hours and tried to outline a short story in my head that might salvage the afternoon.

When I got back to the office, the secretary gave me a funny look.

"Susan [the office manager] wants to see you," she said. This was not big news, but the gravity of her voice made me pause.

Am I in trouble? I thought. My mind raced with any number of things I could have done. Mistakes on expenses? Personal e-mail? I walked past my colleagues' cubicles and to her office, trying to figure out what I had done.

Susan was talking in a low voice on the phone. I peeked in, and she motioned me over.

"Hi," I said. "You wanted to see me?"

"Your mom is on the phone," she said, and handed me the receiver.

My mom? I thought. She and my father had been in Hawaii for two and a half months on vacation. They were on the Big Island for a weeklong bike ride that included a jaunt up an extinct volcano. It was strange for her to be calling. Instantly, I thought Granny must be sick or dead.

"Hello?"

"Hi honey, I have some bad news," my mom's voice said. She spoke in an ultra-controlled, low voice that I have always called her principal's voice: steady, unwavering, effective in cooling a hysterical eight-year-old student or a forty-year-old parent. She was using it with me now.

"Dad had a massive heart attack," she said, then paused. "And he didn't make it."

I shrieked. I dropped everything I had in my arms, my umbrella, my notebooks, all the papers I had gathered at the Senate hearing. I collapsed into breathless sobs.

"No! No! No!"

Impossible. Dad was in the best shape of his life since he had retired the year before. He had lost weight, lowered his cholesterol, and was going to the gym. He had started to pull the collar of hair around his bald head into a ponytail and had seemed younger than ever when I'd seen him a few months before. Dad had talked about traveling with Mom, buying a condo soon, in someplace like Florida or even D.C. He had just promised me that he would put together my wedding album, because he loved that artsy stuff. He was going to be a great grandparent, once his kids finally had children of their own. Sure, he had made me go over their will recently, but I had blown it off, because, well, I never believed that he would die, at least not so young. He was one month shy of age sixty-three and six months shy of celebrating his thirtieth wedding anniversary.

"What happened?" I gasped. I was numb except for the shudders that raged through my body. My mom explained, her voice still cool, that they had cycled up and into Volcano National Park the day before. Dad had been afraid he wouldn't make it, but then he dominated the ride—Mom said he was "dancing" on his bike. He was ecstatic when he reached the peak. The group ate dinner together and then they went to sleep. My mom woke in the middle of the night to loud snorelike noises coming from my father. She was surprised because after he had lost weight, he had stopped his thunderous snoring. Then she felt him wet the bed and she jumped up.

She screamed for help, and the couple that was staying in the cabin with them came running. Their friend tried to force his breath into my dad's mouth, hoping to revive him, and the medics did too. But he was dead.

Mom went with him to the hospital. After the doctors' futile efforts to revive him, she was able to observe the cadaver. It was just that: a corpse, an ashen, bloated body on a hospital cart. It was not Rollie Hopgood, the husband who commanded a room, who rallied his students or his softball players or his union, who stopped at nothing to adopt his three Asian children. Mom told me later that the only time in which the body seemed like him—the man she married on a whim and who always had seemed so much bigger than the life that contained him—was just before they took him to be cremated. She caught a glimpse of his hand peeping out from beneath the hospital sheet. It was healthy and tanned from the Hawaii sun. It wore his wedding ring, the one he had designed with circles and lines. Mom held that hand for a second, slipped off the ring, and left.

I was trembling and crying as she told me bits and pieces of this story. I asked questions but don't remember what. I tried to calm down. My head filled with a despondent fog.

Dad once told us: "When I die, I want to go to sleep and never wake up."

And that's just what he did. He always did what he promised.

WHEN HE WAS still a high school art teacher, Dad used to take Hoon-Yung and me on the myriad extracurricular activities he oversaw. He converted an old school bus into an artmobile during the summers and drove from school to school, entertaining kids. Inside, there were benches and tables where students would work on art projects. I remember sitting in the bus, dizzy from the smell of glue and paint, pasting seashells onto colored construction paper. Dad coached softball and basketball, played and umpired slow-pitch softball leagues all summer. We were faithful fans, eating snow cones and watching from the bleachers.

My favorite outings were the dances.

I would get gussied up in my prettiest little dresses, such as my frilly yellow Fonzie-wedding frock, and my mom would do my hair, often in ponytails with ribbons. She would curl each tail into a little spiral and help me buckle my white sandals. Then my dad, all groomed, would take me to Taylor Center High School. I loved to prance around to the funky music and hang around all those teenagers who fussed over me. The female students took me by the hand and carried me around the gymnasium, which was decorated with posters and streamers and swirling in multi-colored lights. I felt like a big girl.

I waited eagerly for the DJ to play the slow songs, often some ditty like "Looks Like We Made It" by Barry Manilow. Then my dad would take a break from his chaperoning duties and come find me. He would gather me up into his arms and prop me against his chest. I would wrap my arms around his neck. Then, he would sway back and forth to the music. He didn't like to dance, I would later find out, but he did this for me because I loved it.

During my wedding reception in 2000, I felt like that little girl again. More than two decades later, my dad tolerated a full four minutes and thirty-three seconds of Céline Dion's "Because You Loved Me" (though not without grumbling a few times, "Is it over yet?"). As usual, Dad did this to make me happy.

After his death, the world my dad had so consciously and carefully constructed seemed to be disintegrating. The void he and my mom had filled, the one that might have engulfed me after I was sent away from my birth family, seemed to open into a black hole. There had never been a time in my life that I felt abandoned or unwanted or unloved. Now I felt as if I was desperately alone.

When I could compose myself, I tried to be the strong daughter that he would have expected me to be. I quizzed Mom on the logistics: How was she going to get home? How was she going to get their stuff home? Did she want me to join her? She needed to get from an isolated part of the Big Island to the airport on the other side, with their bikes and belongings. She would have to stop in Honolulu to pick up the things they had left in their condo and then get to Detroit. Mom hated to fly and hardly ever flew alone. Dad was usually right by her side, holding her hand when the airplane hit full speed, screeching, before jerking upward into the sky.

Hoon-Yung had offered to go to Hawaii to meet her, too, but she said that wouldn't be necessary; we'd probably be more trouble than help. She wanted to get home as soon as possible and it would take us at least twenty-four hours to get to where she was.

My mom was just as concerned about me.

"Can someone drive you home? Can Monte come and get you?" she asked.

"I can get there," I told her. "I can take a cab. Or I'll wait a little while and then drive." My voice had stopped trembling but sounded hollow, a vague echo of itself.

"I'll talk to you soon. I love you."

"I love you too, Mom. Call me as soon as you can."

I hung up. It was rush hour. I couldn't leave yet. I'd be stuck, angry and hysterical in traffic. I had a story to finish, so I would finish it. My bosses in Ohio and my husband—who was thirty miles away in his southern Maryland office—thought I was nuts.

"Go home, honey," Monte said. "I'll meet you there."

I said I would write my story. What else could I do? My father was dead.

I made it to our apartment, somehow. The traffic swelled around me on the parkway. I don't remember parking the car or entering the house. I do remember changing clothes; I was wearing a black silk Banana Republic blouse, which I tossed aside and never found again. I called my brothers. We agreed that I should head home when Mom got to Michigan. I could only wait. Monte and I went out to eat that night to a bar-restaurant called Hard Times Café in Alexandria, needing a breath of air to avoid being suffocated by grief. We cried into our chili.

When we got home, I sent messages to friends and family, including my birth sisters. Everyone was shocked.

My sister Jin-Hong called me the next day to tell me how sorry she was.

"Thank you," I said.

"Ba wants to talk to you," she said.

Ba was last person I wanted to speak to. I couldn't bear to

hear his gravelly voice, no matter how sympathetic he might be. I could not bear to not understand him, and I could not bear to understand him.

Ba's decision to give me away had been a good thing for me. He once told me that he decided to give me to Rollie and Chris Hopgood because he felt I'd have a better life, but Ba was also the first man to reject me. He would not have given me away had I been a boy. He was the man who cheated on our birth mother and broke my sisters' hearts. Ba embodied some principles I could respect, but he was also a living and breathing example of others that I abhorred.

I could not bear the thought that he was the father I had left.

"Not now," I said, firmly, and my sister understood.

MOM MADE IT BACK to the U.S. mainland after a twenty-four-hour nightmare of flights and mishaps. Some jerk refused to give up a seat that was double assigned to my mother and him in Minneapolis. Then the airline lost her luggage. Hoon-Yung ably took charge of the service arrangements; he stepped into my father's shoes and kept going. Monte and I sped across Maryland, Pennsylvania, Ohio. A trooper stopped us. I explained that my father had died, and he let us go.

"Slower," he warned. "But take care."

We arrived in the middle of the night and retired immediately to my childhood room. Early the next morning, I went upstairs to talk to Mom.

"Come sit down next to me," she said. "Dad wanted me to tell you something."

I sat down anxiously thinking from her solemn tone that she was about to reveal a huge family secret.

"Dad thinks you are getting too skinny or could be anorexic. He thinks it's because of my obsession with weight, and I'm sorry."

I stared at her a few seconds before bursting out laughing. I had lost some weight recently after running a marathon but still ate like a horse.

"I am not anorexic!" I insisted.

This was my dad. He was always worrying about our well-being to the point of being ridiculous.

Dad had not wanted a traditional funeral. Have a party, he had joked, but that was a naïve and unrealistic request. Too many people loved him and had to mourn him. About a thousand people attended my father's funeral "reception," on March 17, 2002—many of the same people who had attended his retirement dinner almost exactly a year earlier in the very same Holiday Inn meeting room. A line of hundreds snaked through the room to express condolences to my mother. My family and I milled about, in a dreamlike-nightmarelike state. The number of people and the stories about my dad's altruism, humor, commitment to education, the union, and politics touched us. He did not feel gone.

I heard someone ask, "Where's Dad?" to her mom. I almost answered, "He'll be here any minute."

Sister Maureen gave a eulogy. She called Dad one of the most spiritual people she ever met even if he did not practice a religion. Hoon-Yung, Jung-Hoe, and I spoke. I knew my dad would want me to be like him, strong for everyone else in that room. As they used to look to him, they looked to us to set the tone for how they should feel about his death. As my mom said to us, "Our family is strong. We are getting our strength from him."

I did not shed a tear during his funeral service, though I cried oceans in the months and years later. There is not a day I don't miss him.

14

THE BOY

Humans are surprisingly resilient creatures. I think of my brothers, abandoned, starving orphans, whom my parents nursed back to health and raised into successful and happy human beings. My birth family made a better life for themselves despite the odds. How could I not get over my dad's death? He would have demanded it of me, of all of us. He would have said in his own jolly and inappropriate way, "Get over me! I didn't do all this work for nothing!"

As time went by, the raw pain of my dad's death faded some, though each big occasion—a wedding, the purchase of a first home, a change in job, a change in country, the birth of a child— was a bittersweet reminder that these things could not have happened without him, and yet they were happening without him. Hoon-Yung worked his tail off campaigning and won in a landslide election a seat in the Michigan state legislature. Jung-Hoe, who was working as an environmental engineer, met a Korean woman at his church, and they married in both the United States and Korea. Mom took control of her bills and her life and eventually began dating. We knew our father would not want her to live the rest of her life alone. We all wanted her to be happy.

I continued to be wrapped up in work, my marriage, and in the old, charming, and problematic house we had bought on Capitol Hill. Irene and I remained in fairly regular contact; she tried to visit me wherever I lived—St. Louis, Hawaii, Washington, D.C. She even attended our wedding in Detroit. I also traveled a couple times to Switzerland, where she took me sledding and introduced me to Swiss carnival. Our visits together were relaxed and easy; her English was better than that of many Americans and we weren't contending with the emotional baggage in Taiwan. We just enjoyed each other.

Taiwan, on the other hand, seemed farther and farther away. I stopped trying so hard to stay in touch with my family there. It was not a deliberate decision, but looking back I think they reminded me too much of what I had lost. Until that moment, I had been able to keep an open mind, to endure their quirks and criticisms, and to take each secret in stride because I had two "normal" parents to return to. My dad had encouraged me to keep a level head, to leave the past in the past, to be thankful for what we had. Now Dad could no longer be a buffer for any raw feelings that festered in me. I knew I had to heal before I continued my relationship with my biological family. So I fell back into my American rhythms, and my sisters went on with their lives. Min-Wei moved to Australia for a while with her husband and two young children. Jin-Hong had gotten a divorce, and Jin-Zhi changed her name to Ya-Ling, married, and had two sons. I knew very little about these major events because we exchanged few letters and e-mail.

It was not until 2004 that I realized how distant we had become. Monte and I were planning a vacation to Vietnam after friends told us how wonderful the landscape, people, food, and the general experience had been. We always loved to travel abroad. My husband had lived in Egypt and Kuwait for a couple years; I had lived in Mexico. We had traveled in Europe, Asia, and Latin America together. Vietnam seemed like a great next destination.

I knew I couldn't visit the Asian Pacific without visiting my birth family. It had been five years since I had last seen them, and despite everything that had happened, I still felt the pull of sisterhood and of questions left unanswered. It had been comfortable to settle back into my old life and let my complicated past and relatives slip away. But I never forgot and I never stopped wanting to be part of the Wang family. So Monte and I decided that we would go back to Taiwan for a week before heading to Vietnam.

MOST OF MY FAMILY came to Taipei in honor of my return. We all stayed with Min-Wei and Jin-Hong and their families, who lived together in an apartment near Neihu Road. Ba and Ma came to meet us and take us to Kinmen Island for a couple days. Ya-Ling also visited with her two kids from Taitung. Monte and I squeezed into Min-Wei's children's bunk beds, and everyone else found a place to crash in the bedrooms, on the floor, and on couches. It was like old times.

My sisters took us to do the usual touristy things during the day: the national museum, shopping malls, pools where we fished for prawns. They made their children perform for us. Xiao Ru played the flute. Tasia danced and sang. Rocco ran around like an Energizer bunny and then crawled into Monte's arms and fell asleep. Each day and night one of my sisters or our parents would take us out to eat at some amazing restaurant or would cook a terrific meal. Treating in Chinese culture is an expression of hospitality, duty, and "face." As usual, neither my birth father nor my older sisters let me pay for a meal, even if I insisted and begged.

All of this felt easy and familiar. Sure, there were times in which Monte and I had to seek refuge in the bedroom, away from the kids, the bickering, or just the sheer number of family members, but reentry was not as tough as I had anticipated. I just had to hold my breath and jump.

"Do you know?" Sister no. 5 asked me early one morning.

"What?" I asked groggily. I had just pulled myself out of bed and trudged into the living room.

"There is a Boy."

Ya-Ling, formerly known as Jin-Zhi, was holding her second son. Jin-Zhi had changed her name because she believed her old name had been bad luck. She went to a fortune-teller who gave her the name Ya-Ling, which she said meant elegance, like a bird that flies gracefully.

She was the perfect picture of a frazzled young mother. Her eyes were heavy and her thick hair—my mother's hair—was pulled back but spraying out in all directions. Her big baby boy was trying to squirm out of her arms. He was wide-eyed and his hairline was set back beyond the top of his forehead. He looked like a tiny balding Chinese man. Her other toddler ran around knocking things off tables, screeching. Despite the babies falling all over her, she wanted to fill me in on the latest juicy family story as soon as she saw me that morning.

"Do you know?" she asked again.

"A boy," I responded, blankly, thinking she must mean her own rascals.

"Ba has a Boy," she said.

In 2003 Ba told Ma that he had been keeping in secret two children from an ongoing affair with another woman. That woman had come down with cancer, and he wanted to bring these children—a boy and a girl—home to live with them.

Ya-Ling told me that Ma was infuriated.

"How could you do this? How could you do this and give away my daughters?" she had yelled at him. Still, as she had all her life, she gave in and let the boy come and live with them. But she did not allow Ba's daughter into her home. *Not after you gave away my daughters.*

"He loves this Boy," my sister said. "More than he has ever loved any of us."

Ya-Ling was living in the house in Taitung then. She said Ba had tried to throw her out of house because she would not accept this son, and she was nine months' pregnant.

I stared at Ya-Ling, amazed. I studied her face and saw pain in her eyes, the shame of having a father who kept doing these things. I felt repulsed and angry. Will this man ever stop? This was not rural China. This was 2004, for crying out loud. How could he not see that what he was doing was selfish and wrong?

You can't make up this stuff, I thought. Each story seemed more unbelievable, so I had to confirm this with another sister. I asked Jin-Hong.

"Who told you?" she demanded.

"Ya-Ling," I said, not thinking anything of it. Jin-Hong, Min-Wei, and Ya-Ling always had been my truth tellers, but this time Jin-Hong's face darkened, her mouth grew stern, and her eyes narrowed.

"How does this make you feel?" she asked, concerned.

"Don't worry, I just want to know the truth," I said. I wanted to scream, *I want the truth!* like Tom Cruise's character in the movie *A Few Good Men,* and I could hear my sisters screaming back at me Jack Nicholson's line: *You can't handle the truth!*

"Please," I told my sister, "you don't have to lie to make me feel better."

She nodded, but I could tell she was angry. Later she would

scold Ya-Ling for telling me. She and other sisters worried that I would feel hurt. My sisters had to live with my father's erratic behavior, but they wanted to protect me.

At this point, the Boy was more scandal than anyone wanted to deal with. He made my sisters not want to go home to Taitung during the New Year, a family tradition. Again, they tried to convince Ma to leave.

"Get out of the relationship. You can move in with us," they said. "We will take care of you."

Still, Ma would not leave him. Her life, her home, and her friends were in Taitung and Kinmen.

I couldn't understand how Ma put up with this man's behavior. I had grown up with a different set of values, to be sure. My own mom could be soft and sensitive, but she was also strong and matter-of-fact; before she had met my dad, she had divorced a man who was unfaithful. My dad had always stepped up when any of his children needed it. My husband was loving, supportive, and loyal, and I would have expected no less. I couldn't imagine living with a man like my birth father, not as a daughter and most certainly not as a wife.

My sisters said they, too, would never tolerate Ba's behavior and would leave in a second. Ba's antics had made most of them resolve never to be treated that way by a man. However, Ma was different. She was too traditional, too set in her ways, they told me. Still, my sisters loved her. If this was what she decided to do, they had to put up with it.

I observed Ma with great interest. I was expecting to see a broken, suffering woman, but actually she seemed much more energetic and happy than I remembered. She woke early and marched around my sisters' apartment, cleaning and exercising. Each morning, we found her flapping her arms, slapping her legs to get her blood flowing. My sisters told me that she had become a regular at a Buddhist temple, and she found solace in worship. She could escape all these things, her past and her husband. She could leave herself behind and be at peace. She had a glow about her. She smiled and laughed more.

"Doesn't Ma look good?" my sisters said, beaming.

Yet this whole son thing bothered me. My sisters feared that I would feel hurt that my father wanted a boy more than he had wanted me, but if anything, each atrocity that my father committed reinforced my belief that I had gotten the better end of the deal. I was flat-out angry at his selfishness and chauvinism.

Would Ba really care if I knew what he had done and what I thought of it? I wondered. I mentioned to Min-Wei that I might ask Ba about this son. She laughed and said, "I'm not going to translate!"

The question continued to nag me every time I was around Ba, who behaved pretty much the same, if a bit distracted. He was still overbearing and overgenerous, making us eat too much and buying me gifts, such as a jade pendant and ring. As usual, he quizzed me on my job and apartment in Washington, D.C. He paid for our plane tickets to Kinmen. He insisted we see the usual landmarks and again bought us an obscene amount of Kinmen's special peanut candy.

Ba told us that he would only accompany us to Kinmen and would head back to Taitung early, skipping my last day in Taiwan. We all assumed he wanted to be with his son instead. During our two-day Kinmen stay, I couldn't muster the nerve to confront him. I had grown to dread trying to talk to him. I couldn't understand his brusque Mandarin, and he always persisted as if repeating himself and pulling at my arm would help me understand. Knowing my sisters' discomfort with the subject, I wanted to wait until we were alone to talk.

I finally got my chance when we were standing in the Taipei airport, after returning from Kinmen. We were waiting with our luggage and for someone to pull the car around.

I asked, "Ba, you have a son?"

He stared at me and blinked, surprised.

"You have a son?"

"Yes," he said, composing himself. His surprise turned quickly to pride. "Yes, he is your little brother. He is six years old."

My head was starting to pound. I felt as if I had opened Pandora's box, reached in, and pulled out one of the demons and wiggled it in front of his and everyone's face. I may have been hurting my sisters and my mother more by bringing this up, showing that I had been told, that I was not ignorant to who he was and what he was doing, but I couldn't help it. In any other place and time, I'm not one to keep an opinion to myself. In Taiwan, I had tried to act like the forgiving daughter, but this time I wanted to express my true feelings.

Ba babbled something else. I think he was bragging about how smart the child was. I said nothing. I did not try to understand and looked away. It was a small gesture, but I thought it was clear: I didn't like what I had heard and did not care to hear more. Ba stopped trying to talk to me. We awkwardly parted ways when my sister and husband returned to the baggage area.

That night my sisters' apartment was full of tension. Everyone seemed angry and annoyed. Sister at sister. Father at sister, because he thought she told me and because she didn't approve. Mother at father. Ya-Ling worried she had upset me by telling me because our sisters had chastized her.

"But they don't know how bad it is in that house," she repeated, "how much he worships this son. He never love us like that. Never."

I told Jin-Hong that I confronted Ba, and she retorted sarcastically, "Did he feel bad? Did he feel bad that he gave up his daughter?"

Later, Jin-Hong watched me from her armchair. She was tired of the fighting, but she smiled. She told me she was thinking about my family and my life. Monte and I received news—right there in Taiwan—that his newspaper was assigning him to Buenos Aires. I would be leaving all this soon, and if I chose not to, I didn't have to look back.

"You are lucky girl, yes." Jin-Hong said to me, nodding. "A very lucky girl."

Ba was readying himself to leave for Taitung, but Min-Wei, the one who as a teen had been so angry and certainly not an ally of Ba's, played peacemaker.

"We are never together anymore," she reasoned with our father. "We are all here now. Why don't you just stay? One night. Mei-Ling does not come home much. We can be a family."

He said no at first. Then he realized she was right. He decided to stay. One night away from Taitung and his son would not hurt.

That evening the whole family—my parents and most of my sisters, their husbands, their kids, and my husband and me—wrapped ourselves in raincoats. Armed with colorful umbrellas, we crammed into several cars and sped off into the soggy night. We went to a restaurant that specialized in giant prawns and sat inside a gazebo, an engorged stream pounding like a great river beneath us. It was pouring rain and the sound of the weather and the water made it hard to hear each other. Our voices slowly began to rise above the din, and then suddenly we were loud, almost joyous, almost like we were eight years ago, when we were new to each other and all the secrets were still locked in a tidy box. The children, oblivious, laughed and squealed. We toasted with juice and tea.

I smiled an enthusiastic smile and took pictures of each sister's family, overexaggerating my enthusiasm, trying to lift the mood. I felt responsible for the tension. One of the sisters snapped a photo of Ba, Ma, my husband, and me with my camera. Ba, as usual, was handsome, stern, and unsmiling. Ma wrapped her arm around Monte and hammed it up for the camera. She looked twenty years younger in that picture, more radiant and more stunning than I had ever seen. Her smile was wide and her eyes sparkled. To this day, that photo is one of my favorite shots of my birth mother.

This is how people live on. Life forces you forward. You can hate your family, you can try to forget, hide, ignore them. Or you can try to understand the impossible people that you are doomed to love. Maybe you count your blessings and forgive.

You can't change your past, but you can choose where to go with what you are given. You make your career and raise your kids with your own belief system. You create your own dreams, your novelties, specialties, obsessions, cruelties, and expressions of kindness. You grow your own brand of love. And then you shower it—a spring downpour, a fall sprinkle, a hurricane—on the generations you propagate. Such is the cycle of life.

We called a brief truce and enjoyed each other again that evening. We gorged ourselves on cold prawns, boiled prawns, grilled prawns, blackened prawns, garlic prawns. We drank prawn soup. We dirtied our nails with spices and prawn shells. We used lemon juice and wet wipes to clean our fingers. The rain pounded and our bellies were stuffed, but the night seemed to levitate a little. Enough.

15

MOTHER-DAUGHTER BANQUET

Buenos Aires, 2006

Almost ten years had passed since I'd first met my family in Taiwan. I adored my sisters, and I was both fascinated with and horrified by my birth father, yet Ma still remained a mystery. I knew that I liked her—at least I wanted to—but I had very little sense of who she was. During my five visits to Taiwan over the years, she had been a kind of shadow figure, almost unknowable. She and I could be standing together, even touching, but I always felt as if a piece of soundproof glass divided us. We could talk and talk, but our words disintegrated upon touching the other's ear, our voices merely a blur of earnest noise. We never really connected. While our biological bond certainly had created a bridge, crossing had been much harder.

I saw my sisters' relationships with her—the fussy, loving, natural back-and-forth of mother and daughter—and I was envious. At the very least, I longed to see a bit of her personality unchecked or hear from her mouth why she felt obliged to stay in a bad marriage. I also wanted her to know me a bit better. Thus far, I had failed utterly in this task. We communicated mostly through small gestures, tender and disjointed—a smile, a joke, a pat on the hand—that were usually drowned out by the rest of our family.

Ma and I were profoundly different. She had grown up in war and poverty; I had had a comfy childhood in a midwestern American suburb. Ma was an illiterate mother of nine who felt powerless as her husband and mother-in-law controlled her life and who pieced together a life from the dregs that fate had handed her; I took for granted things like money, education, and unconditional love. The barriers that divided my birth mother and me were immense, greater than the oceans, Great Walls, and Grand Canyons that separated us.

I knew that if I wanted to get to know my birth mother, I would have to make a concerted effort. Ma had not done so and would not—I didn't think she would even have known how. I would have to be the one to reach out. How to do that, I wasn't sure, until one of my sisters gave me an idea.

It was early 2006, and my husband and I had moved to Argentina. We had lived there about a year and a half, and I had fallen in love with Buenos Aires. So many things about the place charmed me: the passionate and abrasive Argentines and their rhythmic Spanish, heavily peppered with Italian inflection; the marble buildings with French balconies; the sweeping avenues with several lanes of cars weaving, honking, and barely missing each other; the cheek kisses; the dog walkers who could maneuver fifteen dogs at a time; the *cortados* (strong coffee cut with a touch of milk) and warm *medialunas* in the morning. Even though many Argentines called me *Japonesa,* or Japanese girl—the kind of comment that would have driven me nuts in the States—I loved the people. The friendliness of many made up for any ignorance. I traveled with and without my husband, writing about dinosaurs and Welsh colonies in Argentina, Indian land reform in Brazil, and cooking schools in Venezuela. I ate ceviche in Peru and climbed Inca trails near Machu Picchu. I felt like I belonged in South America. The warm culture fit with my personality. I couldn't have been or felt farther away from Taiwan. The motivation I once had to try to be "more Chinese" seemed to all but fade away.

Still, living in Buenos Aires and working as a freelance writer allowed me more time to catch up with my sisters than I'd had while working in D.C., and we began to e-mail and chat over the Internet more often. The Web was a blessing for our relationships. The confines of technology fit well with the real limitations of our natural ability to communicate. Chat talk—short, fragmented sentences and phrases—worked well for us. Plus, we could touch base quickly and at whatever hour.

One morning, my sister Ya-Ling started a chat with me after putting her boys to bed. (Taiwan is twelve hours ahead of Buenos Aires.) From her computer on the second floor of our parents' home in Taitung, she filled me in on the bits and pieces of her teaching job and the latest antics of her two insanely active boys. I asked her how Ma was doing.

Ya-Ling: Ma is feeling better now, she has her life.
Mei-Ling: She was great when I saw her last. Despite everything.
Mei-Ling: She was beautiful.
Ya-Ling: She always goes to the temple.
Ya-Ling: She want travel now.
Mei-Ling: Travel?
Ya-Ling: She want go to China.

This could be it, I thought immediately. *This is something I could do.*

I decided, with Monte's encouragement, that I would dip into our savings and invite Ma and one of my birth sisters who spoke English on a trip to China. For a week or two, I would have Ma nearly to myself. I asked Min-Wei, and she said she was sure that Ma would love a trip. Min-Wei, who was now taking care of the kids full time and had never been to Mainland China, volunteered to tag along.

It was a risk, this adventure. Just as I told myself before that first reunion almost ten years earlier, expecting miracles was unrealistic, but at least Ma and I could spend some time together. Maybe we would make some sort of connection. My other sisters had rallied around Ma all their lives. Now she would see that I could be a supportive daughter as well. I knew I might never again have the kind of career flexibility and freedom to travel like this. I needed to act now, before something unexpected interfered. I had learned from my dad's sudden heart attack that you mustn't take for granted that your family will always be there. I wanted to go back while I could to ask some questions. At least I had to try.

Min-Wei took charge of the China plans, which moved forward in the erratic fashion that characterized anything involving my family. Where were we going? How long? With whom? With what company? How much? It all changed a number of times. After considerable back and forth, we settled on a six-day trip to the southern city of Guilin in the region most overrun by tourists in all of China. I had been there before so I knew what to expect.

I did worry about what Ba might say when he found out I had invited Ma and not him. I didn't want to seem ungrateful or disrespectful, but I knew having Ba along would change the entire complexion of the trip and I wanted to get to know my mother.

"It's best if Ba doesn't know that I'm paying for the trip," I told Min-Wei.

Min-Wei thought my concern was amusing.

"Don't worry," she said. "I'll tell him I paid for it."

I still wanted Ma to know that I had suggested the trip, though, I told my sister. Frankly, I wanted the credit. So Min-Wei told Ma not to tell Ba that I had fronted the bill.

"Don't worry," Ma told Min-Wei. "He won't even ask."

AT THE END of May 2006, I flew to the United States to attend my brother Hoon-Yung's wedding reception before leaving for Taiwan. Hoon, who was now a Michigan state legislator, had married a woman from Korea. Jung-Hoe also had married a Korean woman, a couple years before, and had a baby girl. So in the end, both brothers ended up with women who were born and raised in the country they had left as children. In a sense, they were rediscovering their heritage in the creation of their own families.

A couple days after Hoon's party, I left Detroit and, after a more than eighteen-hour odyssey, landed in Taiwan at the close of the Dragon Boat Festival.

I've never attended the Dragon Boat Festival, though my family tells me it's a blast. It's one of the most important national holidays in Taiwan, aside from Chinese New Year and the Mid-Autumn Festival, and is dedicated to Qu Yuan, a statesman who fought corruption during the Zhou dynasty. Legend has it that after he was exiled and heard news that the Qin had defeated the Zhou, he killed himself by jumping into the Milou River. The people are said to have rushed out onto the river in long boats, pounding drums and throwing balls of sweet rice into the river to keep the fish from feeding on Qin's body. To this day the Taiwanese celebrate by racing elaborately painted dragon boats to the beat of sinus-vibrating drums and feasting on sticky rice dumplings stuffed with pork, salted egg, and peanuts.

By the time I arrived, the races and the festivities were over. Min-Wei and Jin-Hong, who still lived together, came to the airport to meet me, both looking as gorgeous as ever. Min-Wei wore one of her usual hot-mama outfits, a short jean skirt with a tight tank top and heels, and Jin-Hong a slightly more conservative version of the same. I silently noted how stunning these mothers of two looked and I hoped that their postchildren good looks boded well for me.

MIN-WEI AND I met Ma at Taipei's domestic airport the day before we left for China. Ma looked great, her skin radiant and her hair still jet black, laced with only a few gray strands. She wore a white silky blouse decorated with big blue flowers and black and beige checkered pants. She smiled broadly when she saw us and gave me a loose hug as I took her bag. I thought about how in Argentina we regularly and naturally kissed strangers upon meeting them. I got the feeling Ma only hugged me because that's what she thought I wanted; I had seen her embrace my nieces and nephews but never my sisters.

Ma said she had not slept for days out of excitement for the trip and announced that she'd brought sticky rice dumplings left over from Dragon Boat Day and a box of autumn melon and other vegetables from the market where our brother worked.

"Cheaper in Taitung," she told Min-Wei. We lugged her vegetables to the car. Once in the apartment, she made us a lunch of rice dumplings and egg and turnip soup. Then she pulled out the Chinese yuan she had left over from a very recent trip to China and asked Min-Wei to help her count it. As they smoothed the colorful bills imprinted with Mao's face, Ma told Min-Wei she should put away money for herself. Just in case.

"I never did, and look me now," she said. "I have nothing."

Min-Wei told me Ma had visited Suzhou, a city in eastern

China, just a month before. As a citizen of Kinmen, she could go directly to the Mainland from her native island without the special permission that Taiwanese citizens needed, and so on a whim she and a friend went. I tried to hide my disappointment that I could not give Ma her first trip to Mainland China. But in the end, I told myself, the fact that it's the first or the second visit didn't take away from our bonding potential.

The three of us took a nap before Min-Wei's children came home from school. Ma and Min-Wei went to her room, and I went alone to Jin-Hong's room. After a half an hour or so, Min-Wei left to fetch her kids.

Ma and I did not get up. We stayed in separate rooms. The noise from the street filtered in through the windows: the horns and motors of cars and motorcycles, ringing bells and shouting children, water splashing from laundry buckets onto the street. I stared at Jin-Hong's cream wall, beyond which Ma lay in bed. It had been two years since we had seen each other. Yet we weren't comfortable being alone together in the same room when Min-Wei was gone. We didn't know how to fill the silence between us. I realized a breakthrough was even farther off than I had imagined.

EVERY SPRING FOR ten years during my childhood in Taylor, my American mom and I attended a springtime mother-daughter banquets in the basement of Granny's church.

The dinners were simple affairs, but we had to dress up. That was the fun part. I even wore white gloves, which made me feel elegant. We usually picked up Granny from her small one-bedroom apartment little more than a mile away from our home. The men of the church cooked the meals—baked chicken, meat loaf, or some other American classic. The tables were wrapped in Easter-egg-colored paper, and there was often a cupcake holder filled with chalky, pastel mints at each place setting. I was allowed to drink whole milk at these dinners; my mom only gave us skim at home. The pastor spoke, and children sang. My mom secretly hated the stuffy room, the forced conversation, the smell of the musty basement, but for me it was one of those classic rituals of youth, reserved for just my mom and me.

Although everyone knew me as a daddy's girl, Mom and I were close, too. She drove me to all my after-school meetings and classes. She picked out cute clothes. She bought me pads and tampons when I had my first period. She gave me journals and inscribed a short, sweet message in every one. I've often thought our relationship seemed more grown up than other mom-daughter relationships. As long as I can remember, Mom has talked to me as if I were an adult or as a teacher would speak to a student. She is loving but never the mushy, doting type—that was more my father's thing. Discipline was a direct and swift scolding and perhaps banishment to my room.

My mom once told me that when I was about seven, she realized I could probably run our house almost as well as she could. I was boss, like my dad. I went to the grocery store with my dad. I knew how to cut the coupons and balance the checkbook. When I was about eight, I entered a Mother's Day essay contest through the *PM Magazine* television show in Detroit and placed third. I wrote something about being an adopted child and having the best mom in the world. Upon returning home from work one day, my mom was greeted with a bouquet of flowers and a letter saying she would get a *Wok with Yan* cookbook. (It was a hilarious prize because my mom hated cooking. She told me later that she was silently thankful that I didn't win first prize, which would have meant a trip to New York to attend cooking school.) When I was a kid, I always thought of us as opposites in many of the same ways that she was different from my dad. I was outspoken,

independent, driven, and tumultuous. She was orderly and struc-
tured. I was constantly on the go and tended to be ultrasocial, always planning. She liked to be with friends but she always needed
her downtime. I loved food; she ate only because she had to. We
used to fume at each other when I was a moody teen, and at times
we competed for my father's attention.

But as an adult, I started to see that I was more like her than
I thought. We were both exercise addicts; we talked all the time
about the gym and have cheered each other on during marathons.
I, too, could be a neat freak. Like my mom, I had a heightened
sense of smell, and as she used to do to us, I have been known
to noisily sniff my husband. I had come to appreciate more my
mom's sense of humor, her subtle sarcasm, and her quiet generosity. After my dad died, I began to see her outside of his
shadow, as a more independent woman. While we would always
have our quibbles, we were enjoying an ever-evolving friendship. We even took a few vacations together—to Hawaii and to
Miami—and she visited me in Buenos Aires.

Mom thought it was great that I wanted to take Ma to China,
and I'm sure had I asked, she would have given me money to
help pay for the trip. Mom listened with amusement when I filled
her in on the soap opera–like developments in the Wang family.
She knew my relationship with my birth mother had little to do
with us. We will always have our trips, our visits, our mother-
daughter banquets.

MIN-WEI, MA, AND I left for China early on a Saturday morning. My younger sister took charge with her usual spir-
ited aplomb, locating the correct tour group and our flag-waving
guide, listening to directions, organizing our documents. She directed Ma and me to sit in the waiting area while she talked to
the guide. I hadn't seen this side of her when she was in the United

States because I had done much of the organizing. In Taiwan, I felt useless.

Ma and I sat next to each other, quiet for several minutes. Then I gave it a try.

"How do you feel?" I asked in Mandarin.

"Good."

"Sorry for my Chinese."

She shook her head. "Doesn't matter."

"You should learn English," I said, smiling, joking.

"*Buhui,*" she said. I can't. She shook her head and waved her finger in the air. "*Atou. Atou.*" Stupid. Stupid. She touched her temple. "*Hen ben.*" Very dumb.

"Don't say that, Ma."

She laughed at me.

Ma never finished the first grade—my sisters said that because she would take candy to her classmates from her father's shop, she was seen as too playful and not serious enough for school. So she never learned to read or write. Still, Min-Wei remembered that she was quick with numbers. My sister used to accompany Ma to the vegetable market and said our mother could price out in a few heartbeats a bushel of carrots, a head of cabbage, and a pound of onions using just a rudimentary scale and her head. Ma always said that her daughters got their smarts and business sense from Ba, but Min-Wei said she was good at math because of Ma. I wondered if I, too, could have gotten my talent for numbers from her.

I asked Ma if she could read at all.

A little, she said. She could recognize and scribble her name. She could read the most simple of characters, for example, heaven (天), one (一), two (二), and mouth (口). Most of her life, she had relied on her husband and children to translate for her.

Then, in the 1990s, Ma had a severe accident.

My sister had had a premonition. Jin-Zhi was at school in Taipei, and her eye began to pulse uncontrollably; some Chinese believe that when your eye twitches, something bad is about to happen. Her friends said she was being overly superstitious, but she was sure something terrible was afoot. Then they got the call.

Ma and Ba had fought over his attending dance classes, where he held other women close. She had begged him not to go. She got on her knees and pleaded.

But Ba said he wouldn't stop, ever.

Ma was enraged. She walked out, and got on her scooter without putting on a helmet. After that, she just didn't remember. She drove blinded by anger, trying to escape the pain of realizing that she had suffered for a marriage that would never be happy. Her husband was never going to change. Her mind was full of despondent fury.

She hit loose gravel on the road, and she and her bike went flying. Those who saw the skid marks, which seemed to go on for a few hundred yards, wondered how she lived. Actually, Ma almost died. When she awoke, she didn't know who she was. Ma suffered a severe concussion. She didn't recognize anyone and lost her short-term memory for a time. Eventually, after excruciating treatment and therapy, Ma recovered, but she would never be the same, or at least she would never believe that she was the same. She had never considered herself smart, but after the accident, she believed she was even more stupid. *Atou. Hen ben.*

Ma went back to school for about a year to try to learn more characters, but she stopped because she couldn't find anyone to drop her off and pick her up each day. Ba, apparently, was too busy with whatever he was doing. Ma told Min-Wei and me that not being able to read was a burden she was glad her daughters had escaped.

"When you don't understand, it's like you are blind," she said. That, I understood perfectly.

GETTING FROM TAIPEI to Guilin required two plane trips, two border crossings on foot, and four bus rides.

Chinese poets through the centuries have celebrated the otherworldly beauty of Guilin, the capital of the autonomous and mystical region of Guangxi. Thousands of years of acidic rain and pounding winds have sculpted a wonderland carved into limestone and carbonic mountains, with sinkholes, pounding rivers, and more than three thousand caves. Angular karst formations protrude sharply against the blue sky taunting the imagination into perceiving the shapes of camels, elephants, bridges, Chinese unicorns, and old wise men. Underground, miles and miles of stalagmites and stalactites form fantastical cities, which the ever-entrepreneurial Chinese have turned into virtual amusement parks by lighting them up with multicolored spotlights. Guilin is the kind of place that can haunt your dreams, if not for the evocative landscape, for the hordes of tourists and street vendors that swarm every attraction. I was torn between being absolutely amazed by the physical beauty of the place and wanting to jump off of our cruise ship on the Li River for the constant barrage of commercialism. I had been here before in 1999, so I knew this was coming. Thankfully, Ma seemed to love everything she saw.

"How precious," she would mumble, patting the wet wall of yet another cave and tipping her head back to stare upward.

Throughout our trip, our guide—whose name I only knew as Miss Linn—described in depth the myths of the region and the backstory of each attraction and tradition. I continued to understand very little, so I often ended up staring morosely out the window of the bus. Min-Wei deciphered what she could, but she struggled to balance taking care of Ma, translating for me, and maintaining her hypersocial ways. She was incredibly chatty, like I might normally be, and befriended many of the other passengers. She would flit from person to person joking and charming them. I could only watch and smile, enclosed in my dark box of ignorance. Once, after listening for a long time to the guide's talk and not translating a word, Min-Wei turned to me and explained her silence.

"This is history," she said. "Not very interesting."

I NORMALLY LOVE Chinese food, but on our China trip I practically grew to dread eating. I got sick quickly of the breakfasts of greasy noodles, soggy Chinese broccoli and chewy bread, warm soy milk, diluted tea, and watery Nescafé. I longed for a glass of cold orange juice, a scrambled egg, or a piece of bacon. I barely touched the fatty spareribs and spiny fish from the local rivers. We did partake in a few remarkable meals, such as a lunch of different kinds of mushrooms from the Yangshuo region, or a buffet spread in a restaurant owned by a Taiwanese man. But after a couple days, my appetite became uncharacteristically unenthusiastic.

Min-Wei would spoon up portions, and like a good mother, motion to Ma and me, saying: "*Lai, lai, lai.*" Come, come, come.

I put my bowl forward half-heartedly and let her fill it, but I usually ended up leaving much of it to the side.

"You eat like a bird," said the woman next to me.

That's funny, I thought. Most of the time people were astonished with how much such a little person could put down.

Our table company did not make the meal any more appetizing. One relatively sweet little old man routinely around midday developed a case of body odor that could knock you over. Another couple was a caricature of the crudest Chinese people. They burped, snorted, coughed, hacked, sneezed, spit, and farted all through mealtime. Then they lit up their cigarettes while the rest of us were still eating. I knew that these were normal behaviors in many Chinese and Asian cultures. I grew up with two brothers who used to burp and fart and who recently had started to make more noise when they chewed than a dog gumming on a rawhide bone. Yet this couple's bodily expressions were exceptionally loud. They hoarded the best dishes. They picked—or shall I say dug—into their noses in public. I tried to throw them nasty looks when they burped so loudly that I thought that something other than sound had come out of their guts, but they ignored me. They could have cared less what the foreign girl thought.

Ma had her mealtime quirks, too. She let out some pretty impressive belches midmeal and loudly slurped up noodles or soup, as if it enhanced the flavor. Min-Wei reminded her at first to use the chopsticks that had been designated for serving, rather than reaching into the plate with her own as they might do at home. My own mom had monitored our table manners with vigilance when we were kids. We always chewed with our mouths closed, kept our elbows off the table, covered our mouths when we yawned or sneezed and were expected to say "excuse me" if we burped. Loud belching, in general, was frowned upon. We ate mostly healthy foods—we were never allowed to eat sugar cereal growing up and were given candy only once in a while. We brushed our teeth two or three times daily. I suspected that my mom would have been horrified by the lack of etiquette at our daily banquets in China.

Ma didn't worry about being delicate. She basked in the glory of unlimited food, even if she didn't particularly like it. She was a marathon eater. She started out slow but kept on going until the second we stood up to leave the table. She also was a food hoarder. During breakfast, she always helped herself to the buffet after she finished eating, carefully wrapping and stowing away in her purse stuffed buns, sweet bread, croissants, and even hard-boiled eggs. "Just in case," she said.

After almost every meal, Ma and the other members of our group gleefully bargained with Chinese vendors who hounded us, negotiating for fruit and vegetables. Everyone bought huge stems of lychee—which were in high season and deliciously sweet—plums, peaches, and entire melons. They waved their bounty in the air when they entered the bus, grinning and chattering away about how much they had paid. So ten minutes after finishing a meal, we were eating again. When we checked into our hotels at night, many people left their remaining bounty on the bus. So come morning, the vehicle smelled of overripe produce. I pinched my nose to endure the stink. No one else seemed to mind.

MIN-WEI'S FIRST PRIORITY was looking after Ma. She got her documents in order and held on to Ma's money to be sure that our mother wouldn't be tricked into buying false goods for high prices. She vetoed souvenirs that she thought were a waste. She walked Ma to her hotel room each night—Min-Wei and I stayed together while Ma shared a room with a single Taiwanese woman who was traveling with friends—and reminded her over and over which room we were staying in.

The task that consumed most of Min-Wei's attention—and mine, too—was meeting Ma's bathroom needs.

I had my first encounter with Chinese bathrooms during my 1999 six-week cross-country tour. On that trip, we frequented all types of bathrooms, ranging from holes in the ground to Western toilets with fold-down seats. The most challenging and disgusting bathrooms were merely long troughs, over which you squatted with your feet precariously placed on the slick, wet floor on both sides. You and all the other women lined up in a row, butts bared and hung low, the pee and excrement flowing below. Other "public" bathrooms were no more than holes in small wooden huts at the side of the road. Sad to say, that part of China—despite an edict from the government in light of the approach of the Beijing Olympics to clean up public toilets—seemed to have evolved little.

We had no choice but to endure because Ma used the bathroom just about every hour, a need that had vexed her ever since she'd had her operation for cervical cancer. Min-Wei was especially astute at perceiving when our mother might need to go and made sure Ma went before she got on the bus or took a long walk. We became the super-sister bathroom tag team. During the early days of our trip, we three were always the stragglers, the last to join the group, enter the attractions, or board the bus. We soon learned to plan ahead, with one of us running ahead to reserve a good spot on the bus and the other accompanying Ma.

I eagerly threw myself into the role of Min-Wei's humble assistant, escorting Ma to the bathroom, helping her up and down stairs, making sure she didn't wander or spend her money unwisely. I may not have been able to communicate with Ma, but these simple caretaking tasks I could do. Ma was sixty-three years old (or sixty-four in Chinese years because they say babies have entered their first year when they are born). I wondered if she expected or wanted the help we insisted on giving her. Did she think we were patronizing her? My American mom certainly would have.

Whatever the case, I followed my sister's example. At least it helped me feel a bit more like a real daughter.

THE TOUR WAS so rushed and Ma and Min-Wei were so distracted that I had to sneak questions to Ma whenever I could. Min-Wei almost always had to translate because after Ma said a sentence or two in Mandarin, she would switch to her native Taiwanese.

On the plane to Macau: *What did you do as a child, growing up?*

On the bus between guide speeches and catnaps: *How did your family end up in Kinmen?*

In the room as we were getting ready: *When did Ba first see you? What did you think of him?*

After dinner, one night before bed: *What was the war like?*

I obsessed more about when the next opportunity for questions would be than what attraction we were visiting. I was worried that time would run out, and I wouldn't have asked all the things I hoped to ask. I apologized to Min-Wei and my other sisters who were forced to channel my curiosity and questions and confront, in some cases, very unpleasant situations. In the end, Min-Wei reassured me that she was learning about our history, too. So often we live with our parents and never ask where they are from and what their childhood was like. I regretted not writing down the details of the stories my dad or my grandparents told. I wish I had paid closer attention to their lives when they were living.

So I peppered Ma with questions, and she answered as well as she could. Translation was a constant challenge, and her memory was fading and jumbled. She would tell the same stories twice or a few times, and change key details. (*I was in the mountains when the bombing started.* But later: *No, I was in my vegetable patch.*) Min-Wei often had to ask several questions to my one in order to figure out what she meant. In the end, much of what I learned about both Ma and Ba came from recollections from Min-Wei and my other sisters, and I was sure I was not being told everything.

One night before bed, Ma told me that she and Ba had disagreed about my adoption on many levels, despite what both of them had told me during our first reunion. This was Min-Wei's approximate translation:

"Ba believed that if the girls are adopted in Taiwan, the Taiwanese parents will feed the kids, but they will grow up and then get sent to be prostitutes. Not good to be with Taiwan parents, Ba say. They will want the daughter to make money for them. He think foreigner is better. My and Ba's opinion opposite. I think it better to give to Taiwan parents, not foreigners so I can see the kids and I can see that the kids are okay.

"If the kid is sent to a foreign place I don't know what happened to her. Is she have a good life? How does the parent treat kid? I don't know. If we gave you to Taiwan parents, I could have seen you.

"The leader was Grandmother," Ma said. "She say, 'Give her away.' And Father say okay."

Grandmother. I thought of Ba's mother and the few pictures I had seen of her. She seemed small and frail, but she was omnipresent in my family's history. I got the sense that this woman, who bore nine boys—three of whom survived—was the mastermind behind the family madness. She had the final say behind so many key decisions: when to give and not to give a child away, when to adopt one. She was the screech that woke my sisters most mornings, the reproach that cut through Ma's heart, and the whisper in Ba's ear.

Grandmother died in 1996, the year before I was reunited with the family, so I never met her. I didn't know a lot about her, though she received mixed reviews from my sisters. Some said she was mean and told me about how she smacked or pinched them. Others said she was caring, and loved them very much. For sure, both Ma and Ba demanded their children respect her. One sister told me that at her funeral all the girls were made to crawl on their hands and knees around our grandmother's body, crying out in grief. I wondered if Grandmother had been alive and I had met her, how I would have felt about her. I bet she would have seemed amusing and eccentric at first, a sweet and sassy old

Chinese lady. Yet, just as my patience eroded with Ba, I suspect it would have with her. And in the end, I would have had to hide my disdain for the things she had done.

Ma said she believed she had no right to challenge her mother-in-law—always a higher position in any traditional Chinese family—so she let Irene and me go.

"I think if you stay we can still go on, we are not really, really poor. If you were here, you would still have food. We are still here. We survived. We had to eat rice and vegetables, and we couldn't eat a lot of meat. It was not so good, the food, but we could eat."

Min-Wei stopped translating and added her own editorial comment. "I think it was better to send you to another country," she said.

DURING THE THIRD NIGHT of our tour, we stayed in a three-star hotel with 168 rooms in the township of Lupu. The hotel sits above the Feng Yu cave, at the "Fenyu Yanwenoquan-shanzhuang," according to the hotel's badly translated English promotional material. This hot-spring mountain villa is "a good resort for tour, convalescence, having meetings, dining, lodgment and shopping, which is your best choice."

It was indeed pretty, but being a wet mountain resort, it was also a mosquito paradise. We covered ourselves with repellent and pulled our clothes tightly around our bodies in any public room. I covered the crack at the foot of the hotel room door with a towel and sprayed my floppy hat with repellent, which I then wore to bed.

I hate mosquitoes. I despise them with a violent passion. If one is buzzing around my bedroom at home I will bolt up straight out of a dead sleep, switch on all the lights, and stomp around the room with crazed eyes hunting the beast while my poor husband grumbles into his pillow.

Ever since I was little, mosquitoes have stalked me. If there was one insect among twenty people, it would bite me, and the welt would swell to superhuman sizes and leave a scar that would last the summer. When my husband and I traveled to the rain forest in Thailand, he didn't wear insect repellent because I was with him, and they always bit me instead. During my first trip to China, mosquitoes bit almost every part of my body, and the bites swelled into giant red bumps. I slathered DEET-laced lotion on my arms when I went to sleep, and then they bit me on the forehead and chin. The next night I put repellent on my face, disregarding the dire warnings against doing so. A mosquito bit me on the eyelid, the only place I missed. For three days I looked like the elephant woman. During a recent safari in a Brazilian swamp, I received more than one hundred bites from mosquitoes and flies. My friend counted sixty welts on my arms and back; I told her to stop before I had a nervous breakdown.

On our China trip, I expressed my neurosis openly and freely as I slathered 99.5 percent DEET repellent on my exposed skin. I knew well the phrases in Chinese "I hate mosquitoes" and "A mosquito bit me."

"You have my skin," Ma said, observing me. "That's why they like you."

It might seem pitiful to focus and obsess on such a tedious topic, but I found myself groping around for subjects Ma and I could both relate to. Mosquitoes, I could talk about, without Min-Wei's help. Ma and I talked in child-level Mandarin about why they liked us and how and where we had been bitten. We discussed what attracted them and how to prevent them. There wasn't a day that went by in China when the subject did not come up. The three of us chased stray mosquitoes around our rooms together, laughing and cursing.

In Lupu, despite all of our precautionary measures, I suffered a bite on my leg that swelled up impressively, red and hard. Ma examined the bite and shook her head. She held up her finger, as if to say "wait," and I did. Then she removed a small, round container of Green Bamboo salve from her bag and screwed off the cap. She dipped her index finger into what looked like Carmex. I propped my foot on the bed so she wouldn't have to bend down. She rubbed the salve gently on my bite and looked up at me.

"This helps heal mosquito bites," she told me.

"Okay."

"Better?"

"Sure," I said. It was. And for a second I felt that we recognized each other: a mother, a daughter, and a mosquito bite.

ON THE LAST MORNING, as we were getting ready to head home, I tried to wrap up my barrage of questions.

"How do you feel about your life?" I asked.

"My whole life was worth nothing. It was not worth it to marry with Ba. We worked so hard when we were young, but in the end it didn't work out. I gave him everything. I tried to give everyone a good life and never asked for anything in return. My whole life was my marriage. That's just what I had to do. And we have a bad relationship.

"But my life is not too bad. I still can eat and still can spend whatever I want [thanks to her daughters and her own thriftiness]. That's enough. I don't really care what he does now. I can't change things. It's too late. The kids have a good life. That's enough for me.

"Buddhists have to be calm. I want to be a good Buddhist. I don't want to care about anything. I would like to go to the temple and worship more, but I can't read the texts."

"Do you believe you had bad luck?" I asked.

"I don't believe I've had a life full of bad luck, but rather I have a life without hope," she replied.

Ma never thanked me for the trip—or she never said, in any language, the exact words, "Thank you, Mei-Ling."

I asked her several times if she liked it, shamelessly fishing for a compliment. I was needy and wanted to be reassured that my effort was not overlooked.

"Are you happy with the trip?" I asked.

"Yes, I'm very happy."

"I'm happy to be here with you and Min-Wei."

"I'm happy, too."

After we returned to Min-Wei's Taipei apartment, Ma sat down and proclaimed to me, "I want to pay for my trip."

I knew this was a gesture, this obligatory offer, her way of expressing her appreciation.

"No, no," I insisted, as you are supposed to do.

"*Bu hao yisi.*" How embarrassing. "I never did anything for you."

I shook my head.

"Don't worry about it."

She handed me one of the small jars of pearl cream she had bought for each of her daughters.

I went to bed that night and thought about how Ma and I would never truly know each other. Perhaps we could, if I gave up the life I knew, moved here, and gave everything to Taiwan, but I wasn't willing to do that. I had a feeling that no matter how hard I studied Mandarin or Taiwanese, or how much time I spent in the town where I had been born or the island where my parents had been raised, my birth mother and I would never have a fraction of the relationship she has with Min-Wei or Jin-Hong or my other sisters, or that I have with my own mom in the States. Ma will never be able to tell me one-on-one the stories of her youth. I would never know what she preferred to eat without asking. We will probably never bicker or fight, nor will one of us ever say something so mean that the other dissolves into tears. I will never consult her about my insecurities, my disappointments, and my dreams. That kind of special mother-daughter relationship would always be uniquely reserved for my mom in Michigan, and that was fine. It would have to be.

Ma would remain an enigma to me. I would never understand truly why she became the woman she became. My sisters' explanation—"She is a traditional woman"—would have to suffice.

It was a sad resignation, but at least I could say I tried. I had reached out and given what I was willing to give. I do have a few precious memories. I still smile when I think about the time in Yangshou, while Min-Wei and I primped and packed, and Ma lay on her back on the hotel bed and put her feet into the air. She chanted: "We are going to China, China is our home." Min-Wei shook her head, laughed, and translated Ma's made-up tune.

I do that, I thought. I often make up random, silly songs and sing them to my husband or my dog. *I do that, too.*

I think of watching Ma as she looked up and out of the tour bus window and saw for the first time the dramatic lines of the Linjiang Mountains of Guilin. They unfolded like misty giants, craggy and judgmental. The shadows of trees and telephone poles slid across Ma's astonished face. She just smiled and pointed upward at the mountains. She began talking to herself; no one was sitting next to her. Then she actually started laughing aloud and nodding her head. My frustration with the tour group and my crappy Mandarin melted away.

This is what I had come for, I thought. *This is the moment.*

Ma did not notice my staring. She just kept looking out the window, pointing and laughing to no one but herself.

16

THE NAMESAKES

For two years, I heard bits and pieces about the Boy, mostly morsels that I extricated from my sisters and from my Australian brother-in-law. The girls continued to refer to the son that my father had with another woman as the Boy, and occasionally the Child, but never as Brother. Likewise, they told me that they did not allow him to call them Big Sister, as is customary in many families. Titles are complicated and important in Chinese culture. You call your mother's mother something different from your father's mother. Your father's younger brother is *jiujiu* and your father's older brother is *susu*. Your older sister is *jiejie* and younger sister *meimei*; your younger brother is *didi* and older brother is *gege*. Such titles were traditionally expressions of rank and place in the familial hierarchy in terms of respect, deference, and even affection. I liked some of the titles; it was much easier to remember *jiefu* (husband of older sister) than to memorize five different Chinese names. I also knew the significance of being forbidden to use them.

I asked about this during an Internet chat with one of my sisters one evening.

"Do you speak to the Boy? He calls you auntie and not sister, right?"

"He calls me teacher."

"He calls you teacher? Does he know you are his sister?"

"He does not know."

"Does he know that the other sisters are his sisters? Who does he think they are? What does he call Ma?"

"He calls Ma sometime, sometime calls Ma aunt."

"Okay, so does he know Ba is your father?"

"Yes, he know."

"And he knows Ba is his father. So he doesn't know that you are his sister? (sorry, I don't understand)."

"Maybe he is too little, so he does not know this kind of complex relationship."

"I guess not! I almost don't. One day he will."

"When he grow up. It's Ba, does the wrong thing."

"Yes, I know."

"It's poor, very pitiful."

When I called during the Lunar New Year celebration of 2006, the opening of the Chinese Year of the Dog, Ba tried to get the Boy to talk to me. My sisters and their families already had greeted me, waved and blew kisses through the minicam, but the Boy would not; he hid in another room. When Min-Wei sent me pictures of that reunion, I got a glimpse of this child. He was half turned toward the camera, and his skinny leg was sticking out from under the dinner table. His presence in the photo was obviously an accident.

I had not visited Taitung since the giant family reunion in 1998, when my adopted family and Irene's family went there for Chinese New Year. I decided to go after our China trip because I wanted to visit Ya-Ling and meet her husband, as well as see our older brother. Plus, I needed to see Ba again; there were still so many questions to ask him. And, of course, there was this Boy.

If this was the Chosen One, I had to meet him.

MA AND I ARRIVED LATE, delayed by storms in Taitung and Taipei. Ya-Ling came with her youngest son to pick us up. She wore a light blue and brown striped dress and her thick hair loose. She looked healthy and quite pretty.

"I look nice for you," she announced, tugging her toddler son's hand. "Say hello to auntie."

He stared up at me with big, frightened eyes.

"Say hello to auntie," she demanded, and let loose a string of commands in Chinese.

"Hah-low auntie," he said.

We loaded our suitcases into the car trunk.

"Where is Ba?" Ya-Ling mumbled. "He said he would be here, but I have been here a long time and he is not here."

The day's rain had paused briefly and the air had chilled, a welcome break from Taitung's heavy summer heat. During the ten-minute drive from the small airport to our parents' home, we chatted about the China trip, the weather, and Ya-Ling's work as a teacher-in-training.

The city had grown since I had visited eight years before. Taitung still had more farm fields and swaths of undeveloped land than most regions in Taiwan, but those pockets of emptiness were disappearing. The roads were paved, and new developments and businesses were opening in every part of town. A fancy hotel called the Formosan Naruwan, reputedly the first four-star in Taitung's history (it was unclear to me who was giving those stars) had opened, and we would visit it a few times during my three-day stay when we were desperate for something to do while it rained.

When we arrived, the house was empty. Ba's car was nowhere to be found.

"He leaves during the day," said Ya-Ling. "He leave the Boy here. He tell him to watch TV and he disappear. No one know where he goes."

THE FIRST THING I saw when I walked into my birth
parents' home was an eight-by-ten-inch photograph of President
George W. Bush and me.

My mom had insisted on snapping the photo at the White
House correspondents dinner in May of 2004. As an award
recipient, I had been invited to a reception with the president,
and I got fancy for the occasion, with a silvery, formal gown.
The president, decked out in his tuxedo, has his arm around my
shoulders as if we're old chums. Given that I personally cannot
stand most of his policies, the prominently displayed picture of
Mr. Bush and me was a jarring reentry to Taitung. It had been
placed strategically in the front room, in the wood and glass
cabinet that overflowed with unopened bottles of Remy Martell
and Kinmen liquor, rusty toenail clippers, a white ceramic cat, a
roll of masking tape, a plastic gummy watch with one strap cut
off, and piles of other useless knickknacks. Ya-Ling told me that
Ba shows visitors that photo proudly but usually adds: "I did not
raise her. I did not fulfill my responsibility as a father."

The house was in absolute disarray. I always thought of that
home as chaotic, but now it was as if it had vomited up its own
contents. I wondered if it was because Ma had been in China,
or if this was its normal state. The stiff, mismatched wood and
wicker chairs in the living room were covered with children's
shirts, pants, and schoolbags. In the dining room, the round table was stacked high with Chinese bread, tins of cookies, bowls
filled with chopsticks, baby bottles, cans of baby formula and
powder, bottles of soy and hot sauce, and dishes with uneaten
vegetables covered in cellophane. A coat rack threatened immi-
nent collapse under mounds of hats and jackets. In the kitchen,
baskets, plastic buckets, crates, containers, and bags stuffed with
raw carrots, turnips, mushrooms, bean sprouts, and several other
vegetables I did not recognize covered the floor. Two huge re-

frigerators were bursting with frozen foods, vegetables, pork, yogurt, cow's milk, soy milk, and a small package of expensive, bitter chocolates that I raided every once in a while to keep my sanity.

From the screen door, I could see that the backyard was strewn with clean and dirty clothes. Umbrellas and cans of bug spray were stacked on buckets stacked on empty boxes, next to brooms, rakes, and mops. On the second floor, two desks laden with computers and books were crammed in the wide part of hallway that links two wings of the house with the third floor stairs, alongside plastic storage containers filled with books and files and Ya-Ling's husband's musical instruments.

Every inch of that house was an absolute assault on the senses. By now, I could admit that coming "home" to Taitung did not evoke a feeling of nostalgic longing. By now, I believed it was dishonest to try to stir up some kind of fond memory for someplace I had never lived. I had once yearned to know these hallways and these rooms, these smells and these sights by heart. I had imagined my own sisters' memories—of bouncing on beds, of playing hide-and-seek in cornfields, of walking to school together, hand in hand—and wished that those recollections were my own. But now I realized I was glad they weren't, because with the good came the bad, and the bad was morphing into an uncontainable beast.

I put my suitcase on the floor. Ma asked me if I was hungry.

"*Yidiandian.*" A little.

Ya-Ling and she discussed whether Ma should cook, or whether we should eat at a restaurant. Ma wanted to cook, saying it was a waste to go out. I fell into passive mode, knowing that it was the only way I would last three days here. I knew most decisions were out of my hands, and it was best to go with the flow.

A FEW MINUTES LATER, Ba walked in, claiming he'd been at the airport. Ya-Ling looked at him doubtfully, but I gave him an overly cheerful, "*Ni hao Ba!*" and a clumsy hug. Upon entry, Ba immediately handed me $250, for no particular reason. In form, I tried to refuse. He said, as usual, it was a pittance, considering he did not raise me. He gave me a necklace of fake pearls he bought in China (I knew they were fake because I had learned in China how to rub the pearls together and test the grain; these were perfectly smooth plastic). Then he announced that his son was going to be home soon, and that he wanted me to meet him, and that his son was going to call me *jiejie*, Big Sister.

Ma and Ya-Ling watched me, waiting to see what I would do.

I was not sure what to say. I had given this a lot of thought but was still undecided. Part of me wanted to stick with the society of sisters who refused to acknowledge him as a brother, if only to strike out at Ba's loathsome behavior. I also felt the fierce instinct to fight for who I love and what I believe. Yet another part of me, like my sisters, felt sorry for this Boy. It was not his fault that our father was stuck in another era. It was not the Boy's fault that he was all that my father had wanted, all of his life. Still another part of me did not want problems. I came back to Taiwan so rarely and was not convinced that this was worth a fight.

So I said nothing. I just watched Ba leave on his moped to retrieve his son from school. I sat in the living room with Ya-Ling and her boys while they watched *Chicka Chicka Boom Boom* and other DVDs she had asked me to bring from the States.

My mind raced when I heard the voices and footsteps on the front porch, the click of the lock and the squeak of the screen door.

Then he was there.

The Boy walked into the living room, a tall, lanky child of eight, wearing glasses and a lopsided grin. He had olive skin and blunt-cut hair and long legs and arms. He did not look at me directly or address me, but he glanced at me out of the corner of his eye, obviously aware that I was the famous American sister that Ba had told him about. He pretended to go look for a ball, game, or something to fiddle with. Ba barked at him to greet me. The Boy hung back. Ba took him by the arm and placed him before me.

The Boy stood awkwardly, jiggling his limbs, wanting to escape our gaze and the grip of his father. He bounced a tennis ball. Ba pointed to me or, rather, jabbed toward me with his long-nailed finger.

"Say hi to your *jiejie,* your Big Sister," he commanded in Mandarin. "Call her *jiejie.*"

The Boy stared at the ground, and I stared at him. The child sensed Ba was giving him permission to do something special— usually forbidden. The calm, rational Mei-Ling fought internally with every ounce of her strong and opinionated personality. As much as Ba was ticking me off, I saw that this child was no monster. He was not some terrible incarnation of the sins of our father. He was just a skinny little kid.

"*Ni hao,*" I said.

"WEI-SHENG! SAY HI TO YOUR *JIEJIE*!" Ba demanded.

"*Jiejie, hao,*" the Boy said in a small voice, slowly looking up at me. Hello, Big Sister.

"*Ni hao,*" I said again.

Ba let go of the Boy's shoulder and smiled triumphantly. The Boy bolted into the kitchen and upstairs.

EVERYTHING THAT I had heard about the Boy was true.

I had wondered if perhaps my sisters exaggerated Ba's strange behavior, but in fact Ba did have a disturbing relationship with

Wei-Sheng, whose name I picked up quickly because everyone was constantly yelling at him.

Ba and his son slept in the same double bed in Ba's room, which was equipped with a television set and a poster of Tom Cruise. Ba still helped the Boy with his bath. Ba took the Boy to school every morning and dropped him off at home after his after-school classes, often abandoning the child and disappearing for hours. Wei-Sheng ended up watching television, playing games on the computer, or aggravating Ya-Ling's boys. On weekends Ba would take the Boy to the child's mother's family house.

"Wei-Sheng! Take a bath!" I heard someone yell.

The Boy had stripped down naked, and his bare butt was streaking through the house. He was screeching and laughing, while Ba scolded him, urging him to get back into the bathroom. Ba was readying himself for a shower, too. (In Taiwan, parents and even aunts and uncles often take showers with young children. It is not considered strange among families, but Wei-Sheng seemed too old for this.) Ya-Ling and Ma joined in the chorus prodding him back into the tub. Ya-Ling's two boys were howling because Wei-Sheng was trying to scare them. The house filled with the noise of protest.

I sat in the living room, impatiently waiting for the disorder to settle down, and for us to head out to the restaurant. After they had bathed, Ba and Wei-Sheng joined me in the living room, and the three of us sat and pretended to watch television.

Ba asked me: "How do you say 'big sister'?"

"What?" I said, looking up, not quite understanding.

"Jiejie shenme jiang?" How do you say "big sister" in English?

"Oh, oh," I said. "Big sister."

"Ni shou," he demanded of Wei-Sheng. You say.

The Boy stared at him.

"NI SHOU," Ba commanded again.

"See-ah," Wei-Sheng said.

"Big sister," I said again, awkwardly.

Ma was nearby. She said: "Bee-ah Su-sa."

"Beega See-sta," Wei-Sheng said.

"*Hao*," I said. Good.

I smiled tentatively, oddly, and uncomfortably. Ba was making his point, over and over again, that he had won, that this Boy was part of the family, and that I had accepted him, even if I hadn't.

I DID RESOLVE to be extra sweet to Big Brother.

Min-Wei had told me stories of Nian-Zu's innocence, of the times she defended her older brother from bullies. She told me he still gave her a red envelope with a little bit of Taiwan money for Chinese New Year, even though he barely made any.

"I'm sorry it isn't much," he'd tell her. Giving red envelopes is a tradition usually reserved for children, but he relished the role of big brother. Min-Wei had to accept.

Nian-Zu was the only sibling that called Wei-Sheng Little Brother, but it was obvious that the older son was now secondary. Ba was pushing Nian-Zu to marry a Chinese woman who had been staying in Taitung. My sisters were terribly suspicious of this woman and her motives; they said many poor Chinese women marry Taiwanese men for their money. This woman, my sisters told me, already had married and run away from one husband and seemed to care little for our brother and showed little respect for our mother. Later we would find out that Ba may have had a history with this woman, an accusation he scorned.

Nian-Zu slipped discreetly into the house around 5:30 p.m., after finishing his day at the Taitung market, weighing and loading fruits and vegetables.

"*Ni hao ge-ge!*" Hello, Big Brother, I exclaimed brightly when I spotted him. "How was work?"

He was wet from a perpetual layer of sweat and from the rain, but I gave him a big hug anyway. Despite the fact that it had been eight years since I'd seen him last, he seemed the same—same size, same slowness. He acted as if he didn't want to be noticed, but he clearly longed for affection. He seemed to have two expressions: smiling and not smiling. When he wasn't smiling, he looked sour, even ogrelike. When he was, his whole face lit up and his eyes glittered. His eyes became small half-moons and he looked like a child trapped in the body of a giant.

"Oh my God!" he exclaimed in English. He embraced me heartily but let go quickly and headed to his bedroom on the second floor. He returned with a present, a necklace made of amber-colored quartz, which he explained was special to Taitung.

"This is for my *meimei*," he proclaimed. The charm was shaped like an obelisk and filled with tiny bubbly imperfections.

"*Xiexie!*" Thank you, I said. "*Deng yixia.*" But wait. I fetched a yellow alpaca cap from Peru and an Argentina key chain.

"You brought gifts for me?" he said with genuine surprise.

"Of course. You're my *gege*," I said.

And this time we both walked away pleased.

AT MY REQUEST, Ba told me again the story of our family, how he had to support his mother and brother, and then how he and Ma met. He described the isolation of Taitung then, and how they climbed out of poverty into the middle class. He talked about that first trip to Taitung and about my adoption. Ba told me that his older brother, an alcoholic, chastised him for giving me to a foreign family instead of to him, a thought that made my skin crawl. Ya-Ling translated this time, and Ma sat nearby.

While Ba talked, the more difficult questions played over and over in my brain. By then, I assumed a lot about him and his desires, but I wanted to hear him actually say the words. So I just asked: "Ba, why you do like boys more than girls?"

I asked him directly, though gently, using the overly controlled and calm tone I use during tough interviews—not unlike my mom's principal voice. Ma snorted and laughed aloud. I glanced sideways at her, unable to suppress a smile.

Ba looked at me blankly. Then he answered, "I need someone who will worship me after I die. Girls belong to someone else."

We sat for a minute in silence. I wanted to ask him more, to ask questions about Wei-Sheng or the illegitimate daughter he kept somewhere, or if he even cared about his daughters or his wife or about Wei-Sheng's mother. I didn't want to brew tension so early in my visit, so I smiled and changed the subject. We talked like this for an hour or so, until everyone got tired and Ya-Ling got up to put her children to bed. Then Ba moved closer to me and lowered his voice. He began to complain about Ya-Ling, about how she didn't like Wei-Sheng, and about how she even hit him once. I imagined she was disciplining him in the way most of my sisters disciplined their kids.

"She doesn't treat Wei-Sheng right," Ba hissed. "She is not good."

I stared at him. I remembered how badly Ya-Ling had once wanted his love, how she had tried so hard. *How dare you talk like this about your daughter,* I thought. The heat of anger started to build in my face and neck. I was about to boil over. *We are not on the same side, you and me.*

"I don't understand what you are saying," I told him coolly, even though I did.

He continued his harangue.

I stopped him.

"No, Ba," I said. "*Ting budong.*" I don't understand.

I quietly stood up, and walked out of the room.

ON SUNDAY AFTERNOON, while Ya-Ling's boys napped, their mother and I escaped to the seaside for tea. It was a welcome break for both of us. Ya-Ling was both a loving and frantic mother. Her two boys at eighteen months and three years old were normal boys, chasing each other around the house, warring over toys, screaming with joy and calamity. I adored them, but they could be a handful. The older, Yuan-Zhen, was an affectionate and handsome child, with a wide grin and dewy eyes, but he was at a whiny stage, in which the smallest provocation elicited a ear-shattering squeal followed by dramatic tears. The younger boy, Kai-Quen, was a sweet child, mischievous and tough; he could bump his head into a wall and not flinch. Ya-Ling was trying to teach them English from a very young age. She played tapes with English childhood songs such as "ABCs" and "Bingo" hoping they would absorb the language.

It kept raining, but we went to a beachside teahouse anyway. The gray beach matched the gray sky. We sat next to a large bay window on the second floor and ordered sweet fruit tea. Ya-Ling wondered aloud what would have happened if she, too, had been adopted. She said that when she was a baby our grandmother had believed that the rash on her head, the same suffered by a great emperor, was a fortuitous sign.

"Grandma believed that I would be lucky," she said, laughing. "But it was only a skin disease."

Ya-Ling had changed so much from when we had met a decade before. First, there was her name. Both Ya-Ling and Min-Wei had changed their names completely, hoping for a fresh start on their lives. Plus, all of my Chinese sisters had English names as well, which they also changed. Min-Wei was known as Vanessa, Jin-Hong was Jenny. Jin-Qiong was once Joanna, though I wasn't sure if that was the name she presently used. Ironically, I think I was the only one of my sisters who didn't have a Western name. For my family, names were changeable and interchangeable, and identities seemed almost as fluid.

I was relieved to see that Ya-Ling and my other sisters seemed to have shed their need to convince me that our family was *normal*. Our father's obsession had worn them down until all they could do was try to live their own lives, mostly in Taipei and Kaohsiung. Ya-Ling was the only daughter who stayed in Taitung—because she could not bear to leave Ma alone. She said Ba paid little or no attention to his wife. For example, he took Wei-Sheng to the doctor if he barely had a cough, but if Ma was sick he did nothing.

"She is very poor," she said. "If I not there, nobody care for Mother."

"Do you think it is because of the Chinese culture that Ma doesn't leave Ba? Because it's tradition?" I asked.

"No," she said, offering a different opinion from other sisters. "It's just Mother."

She told me one of our aunts left a bad man, too.

"Do you think she loves Ba?" I asked. "She must, right?"

"Maybe. I just don't know."

Perhaps what happened in our family wasn't so exotic or foreign. Ma was like so many women who can't leave men who cheat, maltreat, or even abuse them. They are women who become entangled inextricably in a net of conflicting emotions, who believe these men are the best they can find. Yes, the very strong backdrop of culture and history helped dictate Ma's beliefs about her role in the family, but she could leave. I watched in awe as Ma continued to take care of Ba and and his son. She made Ba's favorite seafood soup. We went to the market and she searched for a new pair of shorts for Wei-Sheng, fussing over sizes and what color he might like. She cooked and cleaned up after both without thanks or complaint. My sisters had said she didn't love the Boy, but she clearly tolerated him and then some. I could hardly believe that she did this purely out of an old-fashioned sense of duty.

I asked Ma if she loved Ba, now or at any other time.

She shrugged her shoulders. "Whether you love or not, it's not important. You just have to deal with it."

BA CONTINUED TO push Wei-Sheng to spend time with me. He told his son to ask me to teach him how to type on the computer and speak English. At one point, I heard Ba ask Wei-Sheng if he wanted to go to America with me.

I sat up straight, shocked, listening for the answer.

"I don't want to go," the child said.

I breathed deeply, relieved, but I wondered what the heck I'd have done if the kid had said yes.

Ba had pulled the same thing with my sisters. He had told Ya-Ling that he would give her money for a new car if she accepted his son. He asked our oldest sister to take him into her home, and my second-oldest sister, the nicest of all of us, almost did. He fought passionately with sisters no. 3 and 4 over his constant failure to discipline or educate the Boy. My sisters seemed to feel sorry for Wei-Sheng but refused to recognize him as their brother all the same. Doing so would be an affront to Ma and everything they believed in.

Ya-Ling clearly did not want the Boy around us. Wei-Sheng liked to annoy her sons, working them into a crying frenzy by scaring them and taking away their toys, but Ba got angry at Ya-Ling when I went anywhere—a museum, a car ride, out to eat—and Wei-Sheng didn't go, even though Ba himself disappeared from the home quite often. I urged Ya-Ling to at least invite the child, hoping to avoid a full-scale war.

Wei-Sheng did not make accepting him any easier. He was

mischievous and badly behaved. He threw balls in the house, broke things, and never picked up after himself. He was not a terrible child—he seemed bright and eager to be loved—but he was spoiled. If he wanted something, Ba promised to give it to him. As a result, Wei-Sheng did not respect or obey Ba either. Ba was constantly calling after him to do things, and Wei-Sheng rarely listened. But Ba hardly ever punished him. If he did, he made sure to make a show of how he was disciplining him.

Once Wei-Sheng tossed a bunch of paper carelessly in Ba's face. Ba said nothing, but I did.

"Wei-Sheng," I said sharply. "You should not do that. He is your father."

More than one sister wondered aloud, including to Ba, whether these children were actually his offspring. After all, Ba was almost sixty years old when this Boy and another girl were born. To me, the Boy did not look particularly like or unlike Ba, no more than some of my sisters. I couldn't tell.

Ba had rewritten his will so that everything he had, almost, would go to Wei-Sheng, according to my sisters. Nian-Zu would get some rental property that Ba owned, which my sisters said was worth very little. The girls and Ma would get nothing.

More than once, Wei-Sheng tried on his own to approach me. He held out a stack of cards and asked me if I wanted to play.

"Later," I told him.

I, too, did not want to be around him. I could barely understand him, I reasoned. Really, I felt the same inner conflict that my sisters did, feeling both sorry for the child and disgusted with Ba. My instinct was not to do what Ba wanted, because he had so little regard for our wishes and feelings. I reached into my heart, but I couldn't bring myself to call Wei-Sheng *didi*, little brother, or to go out of my way to make him feel like family. It would take more time, time I didn't have, time I wasn't ready to spend.

The closest I came was on the final afternoon in Taitung, when Ya-Ling asked me to help my nephews with their English homework. I pointed to the letter and the corresponding picture.

"*A* is for?" I asked, pointing to the red fruit.

"Apple," my nephew said.

"*T* is for?"

"Train."

"*Z* is for?"

"Zebra."

Wei-Sheng slunk up nearby, approaching tentatively but hungrily. At first he tried to butt in and answer before my nephews could.

"No," I told him. "They are younger. You wait until they are done and then it's your turn."

He did. He eagerly sat at the corner of the table and waited his turn. I let him respond as well. And all of us went round and round, reciting the alphabet together.

ON MY LAST NIGHT in Taitung, Ba presented me with more photos of our family. I had seen many of the pictures of my sisters, posing with each other and with our family in their 1970s and 1980s clothing, their big glasses and long hair. Ba handed me a new stack of pictures, mostly of Wei-Sheng.

Two particularly caught my eye. One was a picture of the girl. Until now, I had been fully concentrating on Wei-Sheng, but I had a half sister out there somewhere, too. I examined the picture. She must have been about six or seven. She was perched on the edge of a beige dresser next to a giant aquarium. She was pudgy and her legs peeped out of a maroon velvet dress. She was wearing white tights, dark socks, and shiny pink shoes. I doubted I would meet this girl. I bet my mother and sisters would not want that.

The other photo was of Wei-Sheng. He also must have been about six. Ba had taken him to a studio. The Boy was dressed as a Chinese emperor, in a blue, yellow, and red silk costume, complete with a crown adorned with strings of white pearls. He sat on a miniature throne against an imperial red backdrop. I shook my head.

Ba has gone mad, I thought. He might have been a good father at one time, but he had gone over the edge at some point. He had lost all perspective and reason, and he believed — or at least had convinced himself — that he had done nothing wrong.

"We have another sister?" I asked him then.

Ba paused, unsure. Then he reached into his back pocket and removed his wallet. He pulled out a Taiwan medical card with a picture of that chubby girl.

"Uh." He grunted yes, pointing to her. He then took out Wei-Sheng's health insurance card, and held them both out to me.

Her name was Lin Ruo-Lan, and she was born in 1986 in August, like so many of us. She was being taken care of by her mother's relatives temporarily. They wanted Ba to care for the girl but Ma wouldn't let her come into the home. Another potential casualty of Ba's mania.

"Where is their mother?" I asked him.

"Dead," he said. "Cancer."

I paused.

"*Weishenmen ta de mama bu shi women de mama?*" I asked, playing innocent. Why is his mom not our mom?

He froze again, his eyes narrowing. I sensed some doubt for a split second, doubt that I would approve of his response.

"*Bu hui jiang,*" he said hoarsely. I can't say.

I pushed a little more, pointing to the pictures.

"You like Wei-Sheng best?" I asked him, meaning many things.

He stared at me.

"*Bu hui jiang,*" he said again.

But we both knew the answer to that question.

BA DROVE MA and me to the airport at the end of my Taitung visit. Ma was coming to Taipei, too, because Jin-Hong had asked her to come back to spend some time with her children. Ba urged her to travel with me so I wouldn't be alone. The truth was, I didn't care either way. I just wanted to leave.

I woke up early that morning to talk to my husband via Skype. Wei-Sheng peeped his head around the stairwell, "Good-bye, Big Sister. We hope you come back. I'm going to school now."

I continued to play nice until Ba dropped us off. Ba told me to tell Irene to take care of her mother, who was suffering from stomach cancer (she would soon pass away, a heartbreaking loss for my Swiss sister). I promised that I would give her the message. Ba told me to say hello to my mother, and I told him I would.

"Take care of yourself," he told me in a low voice.

"You, too," I told him, brightly, with a hug.

Ma and I took the escalator to the gate, and Ba headed quickly toward the airport exit and disappeared from sight.

A DAY OR SO LATER, Ma told me the truth about the boy. The Other Boy.

The story I had been told back when I first met the family had been vague. They had had a baby boy, long ago, but he was sick and died shortly after he was born. That was all I knew. I had put the tragedy in the back of my mind.

This visit, my sisters told me that Ma had recently told them the truth behind that child's death. They recounted her story with a great deal of shame. It seemed so damning, I knew I had to ask her myself. So I enlisted the help of a sister one more time to confront Ma. "What happened to the baby boy, the one that died a long time ago?"

Without hesitation, Ma told me.

She had given birth to this son, about a year after my second-oldest sister. He would have been the first son. He was born alive, but to their great dismay he was ill and had a cleft palate. Ma said that Grandmother and Ba decided it was a crueler fate to let the child live a cursed life, in which he would be sick and shunned and could not be a normal functioning member of society. Back then, the Chinese called these children monsters.

They took the baby, laid him on a bed, and did not feed him. Within a few days, the boy died.

Ma's expression was matter-of-fact and unemotional, and her account was short and precise as if she were recounting her grocery list. She said she always would mourn for that child, but still thought she could not have stopped what was happening. She turned her back to us, went about her busy work cleaning up my sister's kitchen, sweeping up the crumbs and hairs that accumulated constantly on the tile floor. My sister looked at me with sad eyes, then went back to her own preoccupations, her children, the housework, and the evening meal. I internalized Ma's account quietly.

I didn't have a choice. Over and over I had heard this refrain, this excuse: Irene's and my adoptions, the affairs and Ba's son. Ma was bound by culture and tradition, my sisters said. I had been willing to give her the benefit of the doubt and tended to let the credit and the blame for the most catastrophic decisions fall to my birth father and grandmother. Still, it was getting harder for me to tolerate my mother's submissiveness. She couldn't shirk all responsibility in the family dramas that continued to rock my Chinese family. By now, Ma knew she had some power: she had refused to take in Ba's daughter, our half sister, for example. Yet she still remained with our birth father and cared for his son. She elected to stay in a hellish situation, in a sense condoning our father's obsession and prolonging the worry and agony of the people who loved her. While Ba's behavior sickened me, Ma's submissiveness, and ultimately her resignation, broke my heart.

I realized that my sisters and I had all been lucky to be girls; the boys whom Ba had wanted so badly had all been damaged by his own obsessive desire. Who knew what would come of Wei-Sheng, whether he would live up to our father's dreams. I wondered if Ba would repent in his old age and be proudest of his daughters. Probably not. I figured that he'd likely end his days with the same tunnel vision in which he had lived much of his life and would continue to believe that the things he had done were in the end for the greater good.

I shuddered, imagining the days after that baby boy had been born. The child clenches his tiny fists and contorts his violet face in a silent hungry cry as he lies on an old quilt. My mother is in the other room weeping, unable to breathe. My father and grandmother are stricken with sadness, trying to go about their daily chores, convinced that they are doing the right thing but deep inside aching, dying a little, too. They would have prayed to their ancestors to care for the baby's spirit, to forgive them for what they have done. The house trembles with the ever-weakening cries of a baby.

I wondered if our family would pay somehow for what it had done. As the Chinese say, no debts go unpaid in heaven.

17

THE LUCKY EIGHT

Taipei, June 2006

Jin-Hong, along with Min-Wei and Patrick and their two kids, lived in an apartment in a residential area at the foot of Yang Ming Mountain. Their apartment was on the fifth floor of a building that had no elevator. Patrick cheerfully lugged our suitcases up and down the staircase. The three-bedroom apartment was spacious by Taiwan standards and quite modern. My sisters had powerful air-conditioning in every room (something I had longed for on so many other visits), and Jin-Hong even had a plush, Western-style Sharspia mattress (as opposed to the usual rock-solid Chinese bed). She also had an awesome Japanese-style toilet with a seat that warmed up with a touch of a button. Pictures of Min-Wei and Jin-Hong with their kids and friends—my family loves to pose with their index and middle fingers thrust forth in the victory sign—lined the ledge of the living room window. There were no pictures of our entire family together.

I spent one more week with Min-Wei and Jin-Hong, and one by one my other sisters and their families came to see me. By now our visits had become rather routine, a change that I welcomed. I did very little touring in Taiwan. Mostly I just hung around the house with the girls, helping to clean and fold clothes, shopping at Carrefour, dropping the kids at school—the normal things that families do. We did sometimes go out at night or on the weekend, for example indulging at my favorite dumpling shop in the world or looking for Asian-style clothing. Min-Wei took me to her Latin/hip-hop dance class, and her husband treated us to big cups of bubble milk tea. One night, I took some of the family to the most expensive TGI Friday's dinner I have ever bought. The price of an exotic American meal was more than double what I'd ever pay in Detroit or D.C., but after the China trip I was dying for anything familiar.

Afterward, on our way out of the mall, my sisters and I admired a clingy, semi-see-through turquoise negligee and matching panties that hung on the rack in one of the department stores.

"Pretty sexy," Jin-Hong proclaimed. I laughed and turned my back to check out some shoes. The next thing I knew Jin-Qiong, my second-oldest sister, had bought the lingerie for me. We took the gift back to the apartment, and each tried on the nightie, one by one, slipping it over our own undergarments and then strutting through the living room as if we were models.

On the night before I left Taiwan, Jin-Hong asked me about all the things I had seen and heard during this visit and visits prior.

"How do you feel about our family?" she asked.

"I think Ba has gone crazy," I said. "But I was not raised here, so it is easier for me. I did not have to grow up with him.

"I feel closest to you, my sisters," I assured her.

"But you feel something with Ma, don't you?" she asked hopefully. I realized that she and the other sisters wanted me to feel the same protective kinship with our mother. I did, but I knew it was different.

"Yes, yes," I said. "But it's difficult because of the language."

"Yes, I know."

Later, before we fell asleep in Jin-Hong's bed, she inspected me for a minute.

"It's nice that we stay close even if we don't talk that often."

"I think so, too," I said before we both fell into a sound sleep.

WE HAD TO LEAVE the apartment in the wee hours of the morning for the airport because I had an early flight. Bleary-eyed and quiet, we strapped ourselves into my sister's Peugeot. Saying good-bye was still bittersweet despite my desperate desire to get back to the United States, Argentina, or wherever I considered home.

We pulled out of Jin-Hong's neighborhood, and she asked for a final time, "Are you hungry?" as we passed the store where we often bought warm soy milk, tofu, and egg pancakes for breakfast.

"No. I can get something at the airport."

This time, Jin-Hong did not insist; even she was too tired for the usual formalities of being a big sister.

At the airport, I got out of the car and slung my carry-on over my shoulder. We smiled at each other warmly, both exhausted. This would be a quick farewell, just her and me. Ma and Ba were back in Taitung. Min-Wei had gone with her kids to Australia to spend a couple months with her in-laws. My other sisters had retired to their respective homes all over Taiwan.

"You must visit me in Argentina," I said.

"I will try," she said. We kissed and hugged, and I pulled my gift-laden bags into the airport.

This trip had been especially challenging: struggling through the China tour with Ma, meeting this half brother in Taitung, dealing with Ba. I always end up asking myself why I keep reinserting myself into this complicated situation, which is so much more difficult than my own comfortable life far, far away. The truth is, I asked for this. I am the one who kept coming back for more. I put more time and energy into keeping in touch. I planned visits and begged them to come and visit me. I asked the tough questions. I could have left those first impressions smooth and untouched, but I made waves instead. Why had I needed the ugly truth, and why did I stick around once I knew? Was it a deep-seated need to be part of this family? Was it an attempt to know myself better? Was it journalistic curiosity? Perhaps it was all of the above.

The enchantment and intimacy of sisterhood seduced me, made me stay when otherwise I might have fled. I sometimes feared that my sisters thought of my visits as a burden: translating, entertaining, cooking, finding me a bed to sleep in, shuttling me around. I know how taxing guests can be, no matter how much you love them. My visits force them to get together, and my presence and my questions call forth memories that they have tried their entire lives to forget. Thankfully, my sisters always treat me with a huge helping of patience and hospitality. They consider me one of them.

I still wonder what it would be like to actually speak the same language, to live in the same country. These women might snipe, nag, fight, judge, or take one another for granted, but they are ultimately allies. They rallied behind each other and our mother, who they believe is an immutable product of traditional China.

And I still sense a trace of love for Ba. From him they inherited their brains and business sense, their passion and temper, and the same stubborn strength that has helped them rise above his indiscretions. He pushed them to get educated, paid for their college. They might hate what he has done to our mother, but he is their father, the only one they have known. Almost all of my sisters converged on Taitung in 2007 to celebrate our father's seventieth Chinese birthday because they knew it would make him happy to have all his children there. In a funny way, Ba's lunatic behavior helps to unite us. We are all distinct products of this man's muddled logic. I am finding that tragedy is as strong a bonding agent as triumph—maybe even stronger. As we gossip about the last unbelievable thing that Ba did, we are joined in our amusement, horror, shame, and despair. We endure him and our past, together.

While my own feelings for my birth parents are at times ambiguous, I admire my sisters. These women changed the course of their own destinies, took the hand they were dealt and made their own full house. They transcended luck and found fortune in themselves. I can't help but want to be a part of this circle. Sometimes I feel badly because I will never fully be part of their lives. I will not be there as my nieces and nephews grow up, learn to read, play the flute in concerts, or graduate from school. I will always be some distant and exotic auntie, sister, and daughter. That reality makes me feel nostalgic, sad, and glad all at the same time.

"It is good," Min-Wei said to me once. "You can visit us here, but you grow up in America. The best of both worlds."

I BOARDED NORTHWEST AIRLINES flight 70, physically and emotionally exhausted as only a trip to Taiwan can make me. I settled into my aisle seat and waited to hear the flight attendant's voice direct our attention to the seat pocket in front of us and the nearest emergency exit. I scanned the movie and the music selection, cursing the airlines for growing ever more cheap. I hoped to sleep anyway.

I thought of the many plane rides I've made in my life, for vacation, for school, for work, for love, and then I thought of all the trips that my family, in all of its many forms, has made, then and now, crossing land, sea, and the globe, searching for a different life, a new perspective, peace of mind, a place to call home. The list of departure and arrival cities seems endless: Kinmen, Taitung, Taipei, Taylor, Zug, Seoul, St. Louis, Honolulu, Brisbane, Washington, D.C., Guilin, Buenos Aires, and on and on. We have both chosen and been forced down so many paths and found ourselves in so many diverse destinations, but with every journey and turn each of us has woven part of a collective tapestry so intricate that one string cannot be untangled from the other. Reunified, we are a remarkable road map of fate. We are the branches of destiny starkly revealed, hilarious and heartbreaking, with our own special scars and beauty marks.

I imagined my first trip thirty-two years before from Taiwan to the United States.

The airline hostess is en route with me weighing heavily in her arms: a chubby, smiley, gurgling baby. A head full of black hair, cheeks round and smooth. Eyes charged with laughter and, at times, fury. I am charming and irritating my fellow passengers alternately with my giggles and shrieks. As the plane leaves Taiwan, the woman coos, rocking, singing, amusing. It's a long ride, almost twenty-four hours, but she is used to this. The young woman often accompanies children flying solo on journeys around the world. She is paid by the anxious parents to do it. She feeds the children, changes their diapers, carries them, and holds their hands. She dries their tears and plays their games. She accompanies them to their new port and hands her tiny charges over to the appropriate responsible adult.

The airline hostess feels a bit like the stork of Western cartoons that delivers babies suspended in a handkerchief, the ends delicately tucked into its beak. She searches my face for any recognition of the immensity of what is happening. I drool.

The woman doesn't know that I am the sixth daughter of a Chinese farmer and his wife. I could have grown up in the sweltering humidity of Taitung, eating rice porridge for breakfast, learning Chinese script, and toiling in the sun under my father's watchful eye, or I could have been given to an alcoholic uncle who had no wife and no children and who desperately wanted his own family. I could have been engulfed by the secrets of my own house, burning incense in honor of my ancestors. I could have gone on to college in Taiwan, studied English on the side, and scrambled to build a life in a small apartment in the cramped city of Taipei.

Instead, I am on a new route.

Within hours I will belong to different parents, and I will live in a ranch home in a blue-collar suburb where being Chinese is exotic. My parents will teach me that I can do anything and I will beat myself up trying to do just that. I will speak and write English first, and the latter will become my profession. Everything I will come to believe about myself and the world will contrast with the one belief that has driven me from my native land and into a new one: that a boy is intrinsically better than a girl.

While the twists of fate in most people's lives are often imperceptible, or so sudden that there is no time to comprehend their impact until long afterward, this is an extraordinary, prolonged moment. I am suspended high above the Pacific Ocean, between countries, between families, between destinies.

"Ooooh," the tired passengers say, despite themselves. "How old is she? What is her name? Where is she from? Is she yours?"

The woman responds, "She is Mei-Ling. She is eight months old and from Taiwan. And, no, she is not mine.

"She is going to live in America."

↬ EPILOGUE ↫

My husband and I wanted to find out our baby's sex as soon as we could.

This was not for any particular reason. Monte and I knew we would love a boy or a girl the same—we were just too curious and impatient to wait the full forty weeks of pregnancy to find out. We wanted to brainstorm possible names, to buy outfits, to have a mental picture of what parenthood might be like.

A routine ultrasound was scheduled for April 25, 2007, when I was about eighteen weeks pregnant. Monte and I walked several blocks to the appointment, and my heart was in my throat because I had suffered a miscarriage the year before. First and foremost, we wanted to be reassured that things were going smoothly.

The doctor-technician was an older man with a gravelly voice and a formal manner, who shook our hands and called me *señora*. He kept pleasantries to a minimum and told me to lie on the examining table. I unzipped my already-unbuttoned jeans, and the doctor smeared slimy gel all over my belly. My husband sat next to me, squinting at the ultrasound monitor. We silently waited while the doctor examined, slowly and meticulously, the head and spine of the baby and measured the heartbeat. The baby was thriving, to our relief. Then the doctor asked in Spanish, "Do you know the sex?"

"No, no," I said eagerly. "We want to know . . ."

"Let's see," he said, clearing his throat. He placed the paddle on the lower left side of my abdomen. The cloudy, psychedelic images pulsed on the screen. He paused.

"*Es una señorita,*" he said, definitively.

"Are you sure?" I asked, and he repeated it again. Without a doubt.

It's a girl.

Tears sprang to my eyes, even though neither my husband nor I could make out any of the female parts on the ultrasound monitor that the doctor insisted were so obvious. I immediately imagined buying our baby dresses, putting her hair in firecracker ponytails, and watching her fall madly in love with her daddy, like I did mine. I was breathless with wonder: *a girl*. It was one of the most pure and simple feelings of joy I have ever experienced.

I thought later of how different that revelation must have been for Ba and Ma.

They did not have the luxury of elective ultrasounds in 1973. My mother would have had to feel me growing, tumbling, and stretching inside her for the full nine or ten months, wondering anxiously if she would bear a boy and finally feel whole as a mother and wife. The question of gender must have loomed large in that operating room, when Ma was moaning and crying out in pain, urging me into the world. Then came the last push and the fateful announcement, the one that had been repeated to them over and over.

"It's a girl," a doctor or nurse might have said overly brightly. Maybe they even called me healthy or beautiful to gloss over the news that the hospital staff knew was disappointing.

Yet there was no disguising the truth: I was another in an endless string of losing lottery tickets. I don't think Ma held me in her arms. I know she never fed me a drop of her milk. For her and

Ba, my birth was not joyful but rather a source of disillusionment and sorrow, one of many open wounds that would ache for decades. Fortunately for me, my birth was the break my American parents had longed for, a turning point.

Now that I have my own daughter, I ask myself, *Could I have given her up?*

Sofia was born on September 7, 2007. After a dozen sets of pushes, she burst into our world, and my obstetrician lifted her triumphantly. Skinny limbs dangled from her sleek, grayish purple body like spaghetti. Once the doctor cut the umbilical cord, she let loose a desperate wail. A nurse put her shuddering body on my chest, and I wept. After a few seconds, they whisked her away, and the nurses, followed by my husband, went to clean and weigh her in another room. The midwife returned to the delivery room to report that Sofia had a head full of hair, my Asian eyes, and my husband's detached earlobes. I couldn't wait to get to our hospital room so I could inspect our baby for myself, to hold, feed, and take care of her.

What if a fleeting minute with my daughter had been all I was allowed? I gaze at my chubby girl now, charmed to pieces by her gummy grin, and I can't imagine that someone else could or would take better care of her. Could I have given up my child to strangers in a far-off country with only the vague promise of a better life? Before I had my own child, I think it was easy for me to shrug off Ba and Ma's sacrifice as simply for the best because that's the way things turned out. Now I see how difficult that decision must have been for them.

I also can't fathom how Ma didn't do anything to save her son so long ago. My own baby's hunger cry is heartbreaking; I hear it and go running, unlatching my nursing bra in midstride. I realize that Ma was young, scared, and trapped in a mind-set that seemed insurmountable. But she should have risen up—for the sake of her child. I have to stop myself from judging her failure with scorn or even disgust. I try to follow my siblings' example and accept Ma as she is. It does me no good to dwell on the rights and wrongs of my birth parents; I could get stuck in that pit and keep sinking. So I make a choice to forgive and move on.

Lately, I have less time to keep in touch with my Chinese relatives, and vice versa. Occasionally, my sisters and I send each other pictures of our kids or exchange a few e-mail or instant messages. Our contact is minimal, though it's not much less than I talk to my brothers in Michigan. I did have pangs during my pregnancy, when I wished that I could ask Ma about how her body behaved when we were in her belly (one of few parenthood-related subjects that my mom couldn't help me with). Did Ma get stretch marks? How much weight did she gain? But making that call was too daunting: figuring when she and someone who could translate might be home, fumbling through the conversation, and confronting again our lack of a relationship. Instead, I quizzed my sisters on their pregnancies. A few months after Sofia was born, Ma and I spoke for the first time in a year and a half. She was visiting Taipei, and my brother-in-law asked me to hook up a Web camera to my computer in Argentina so that Ma could see her newest grandchild. We waved while my birth mother cooed, "*Hao keai.*" How cute. One day we will return to Taiwan. I think it will feel good to see Ma hug my child for the first time. Maybe Sofia will learn some Mandarin so she can play with her cousins and mind her aunties. Ba might even hold Sofia, although I know I will wish that it was my dad instead.

I always tell people that I found my birth family by accident, that one sentence written in a Christmas card set off a chain of events that I still find mind-blowing. Most days, I'm glad I asked the questions that most adopted children never get the chance to ask. Most days, I like the eccentricity and complexity of my past.

Now I offer my voice to the chorus of ancestors. I am not the son who can perpetuate the family name, but I can tell our story. I am not the heir that Ba wanted, but I, too, can be a keeper of our history. I choose to continue the narrative in my own way, using what I've learned to build our family. One day my husband and I hope to adopt. Giving our children even a fraction of the love and generosity that my mom and dad shared is the best legacy that I can think of leaving. Mostly, though, I've just really enjoyed parenthood and watching Sofia grow.

As I write this, my daughter is exactly seven months and three weeks old, the same age I was when I left Taiwan. She is a couple centimeters longer and weighs a pound less but has the same impressive quantity of brown hair that I had, if a few shades lighter. I watch for signs of everyone in her. I hope she will get my dad's compassion, my mom's athleticism, and my husband's good humor. I already sense that she has inherited my Chinese family's love for eating. To me, Sofia looks more like Monte, but I am amazed at how intimately the rhythms of mother and child are intertwined. I make funny faces, Sofia giggles. When she is sick, I catch her cold. If she is sleepless, so am I. I am keenly aware that what I do now will help build the foundation of who she will become. So we eat vegetables and play and dance. I speak to her in English, Spanish, and even throw in a few words of Mandarin. We read together almost every day. I sit in bed with Sofia balancing in my lap, surrounded by fantastic tales of hippos, bears, and dinosaurs. Then I open a book and let her turn the page.